SAFE
and
SECURE

The Loving

Parent's Guide to

Child Safety

Christina Elston

BERKLEY BOOKS
New York

This book is an original publication of The Berkley Publishing Group.

SAFE AND SECURE

A Berkley Book / published by arrangement with the author

PRINTING HISTORY
Berkley trade paperback edition / February 1998

The Putnam Berkley World Wide Web site address is http://www.berkley.com

ISBN: 0-425-16231-1

BERKLEY ®
Berkley Books are published by The Berkley Publishing Group,
a member of Penguin Putnam Inc., 200 Madison Avenue, New York, New York 10016.
BERKLEY and the "B" design are trademarks belonging to Berkley Publishing Corporation.

PRINTED IN THE UNITED STATES OF AMERICA
10 9 8 7 6 5 4 3 2 1

SAFE
and
SECURE

The Loving Parent's Guide to
Child Safety

FOR MOM

Special thanks to:

Norbert and Lauren

Betsy Amster

Ruth Entwistle

Virginia Lares

My friends and colleagues at *L.A. Parent* magazine

All the organizations and individuals who provided information and assistance

CONTENTS

CONTENTS

INTRODUCTION

I could probably save myself the trouble of writing many of the chapters in this book with the simple phrase "There is *no substitute* for parental supervision." (Easy for me to say: I am the mother of one six-year-old child who still dotes on my company, with a small, single-story house and a husband who actually helps with the parenting.)

Your need for precautionary measures decreases as the amount of time you are able to spend supervising your child increases. And the more children, rooms, and other obligations you have, the more you need to do to prevent accidents.

But there are some dangers that are just too big to gamble with, and some no amount of supervision can defeat. You must guard your child against these. And since hovering directly over your child every minute probably isn't healthy for either of you, a certain amount of danger-proofing is prudent in any home.

Some people prefer to think that accidents won't happen to their child, or that childproofing equals paranoia. But I take this stuff pretty seriously. Accidents kill 6,700 children in the United States *every year,* making them the number-one cause of death in children under fourteen. I can assure you that none of the people who love these children thought they would die the way they did. No one purposely put these children in danger.

These kids died because someone wasn't careful enough. Someone didn't fence a swimming pool, put away the matches, buckle the child into a car seat, or pick up a plastic bag. Someone left a baby alone in the bathtub for "just a second," left a window open, or forgot to put away a bottle of pills. Someone let these kids get into deadly situations. And I think parents who don't keep hazards out of their children's way are gambling with their kids' lives.

But no matter how thoroughly you childproof, you've only done half the job if you haven't taught your child about the dangers she may encounter, and what to do (or not to do) about them. This is vital because someday your son or daughter *will* encounter a bottle of pills without a childproof cap, or a stove that hasn't been cordoned off by baby gates and plastic shields. If you haven't taught the kid that pills are poison and the stove is hot, you could both be in for real trouble. A kid with common sense and good judgment is always safer than one who has spent most of his time behind a baby gate.

So childproof your home, but on the way, stop and explain to your child *why* you are doing these things and just *what* you are trying to protect her from.

But don't scare her, or yourself. Entire generations, including mine, have managed to make it to adulthood without much of the knowledge and many of the safeguards we take for granted. My mom never even heard of car seats or cabinet latches, only made us buckle our seatbelts if we were headed for the freeway, and thought asbestos was good. And here I am—safe and secure.

And someday, your children will also reach adulthood safely. Getting them there is like any other part of parenting: Gather the best information you can, do your best with it, and give them lots of love.

HOW TO USE THIS BOOK

Do not sit down and read this book straight through. If you memorize every statistic and try to implement every childproofing technique at once, you'll drive yourself and your family crazy. You may be safe, but you'll never have any fun again.

Instead, look at the sections that match your concerns and choose the safety suggestions that fit your family. Where several options are available to guard against a hazard, I have tried to list them all, giving more space to those I feel are simplest, cheapest, and most likely to work in real family situations. (For instance, taking those cleaners out from under the sink and moving them out of reach saves you a trip to the store for a cabinet latch, the expense of the latch, the aggravation of trying to install it, and the effort required for remembering to use it.) Use the ones you like best.

If you are approaching the task of childproofing your home for the first time, take a look at the childproofing checklist for your child's age, and refer to the chapters you find listed there (words in bold type indicate a corresponding chapter in the A–Z guide). It's also a good idea to look at the chapters covering the various rooms of the house (child's bedroom, parents' bedroom, bathroom, kitchen, family room) and the sections on environmental hazards (asbestos, carbon monoxide, lead, radon, safe drinking water) to get an idea of the safety measures you'll need to take.

As your child approaches a new age/developmental stage, move on to the next checklist to keep your safety efforts current. As with all else in parenting, it's a good idea to stay one step ahead of your child.

When specific concerns/occasions arise, such as a new computer in the home, an airline trip, the need for child care, or a visit to grandma's, you'll find helpful information under the appropriate heading in the alphabetical guide.

Almost all of the information contained in this book is available free to the public. At the end of each chapter, you'll find a resource section listing the books, documents, or pamphlets I used as sources, and, in most cases, the telephone number or address of the group, organization, or agency that supplied them. If you need to gather more extensive information on one of the topics I've covered, these telephone numbers are a good place to start. The people at these organizations are usually in the business because they care about children's safety, so they're happy to help.

SAFE and SECURE

The Loving Parent's Guide to Child Safety

Section I

CHILDPROOFING CHECKLISTS

BIRTH TO 6 MONTHS

Any safety hazard your child encounters at this age will probably be brought in range by a member of the family, another caregiver, or you yourself. So it is important to stop and think before you put your baby down, give her a bath, or hand her a toy.

What to do

- Your baby will need a safety seat for any trip in the **car**, even the ride home from the hospital.
- Make sure your **child's bedroom** and your home are free of small objects that the baby could swallow, and keep dangerous items like plastic bags well out of reach.
- Your baby's crib or bassinet should have a sturdy bottom to prevent tipping, and slats no more than 2 3/8 inches apart. Beware of used cribs that might not meet current safety standards.
- Always put your baby to sleep on his back, on a firm mattress, and avoid using too many blankets. This has been shown to reduce the risk of SIDS.
- Don't put necklaces on the baby, or attach pacifiers or other toys to the baby with a string or cord. Make sure your baby's **clothing** is free from cords or drawstrings that could become wrapped around her neck, or small decorations that could be pulled off and swallowed.
- When **diapering**, avoid the use of baby powder, which is dangerous if inhaled, and other products that could irritate baby's delicate skin. Never leave your child unattended on the changing table, or any other surface above floor level.
- Take care when preparing your baby's **food** or formula. Make sure everything that comes in contact with the food has been disinfected. If heating food or formula in a microwave oven, be sure

to stir it thoroughly and check carefully for "hot spots." Make sure all solid foods are mashed, ground, or soft enough to swallow without chewing.

- Never leave your baby in an **infant seat** on any surface above floor level.
- If your baby uses a **pacifier**, check it regularly for signs of wear and tear.
- Never leave your baby alone with **pets** of any kind. Avoid having reptiles as pets until your child is at least five years old.
- If you use a **playpen**, make sure the mesh holes are no larger than one-quarter inch, never leave the sides down when your baby is in the playpen, and never tie toys across the top of a playpen.
- Don't leave your baby unattended in **shopping** carts.
- Make sure **strollers** or carriers are sturdy, with no sharp edges that could hurt your baby.
- Keep babies under six months old out of the **sun**.
- Avoid using baby **walkers**.
- Keep **window** cords away from the baby's crib, or anywhere the baby can reach.

Toy Guidelines

This is the time when your child will begin to be interested in toys for the first time. Providing a set of soft blocks is a good way to encourage the ability to stack and build in children four months and up. This set should contain no more than six blocks (all your child can really keep track of at this age) and should be made of cloth or rubber. Avoid wooden blocks, or any block small enough to fit completely in your child's mouth. Any toy you give your child at this age should be light enough so he won't hurt himself if he hits himself in the head with it. Toys should be washable, and free of any part that could pinch fingers, pull hair, or break off and pose a choking hazard. There should be no glass or brittle plastic parts, and no sharp edges. Dolls for this age group should have no deco-rations or accessories, and no movable parts. Crib and play gyms are fine to attach across the crib for babies aged three to five months, but be sure to remove them as soon as your baby can pull himself up. Babies can strangle if they become tangled in these toys. Mobiles should always be hung out of reach of your child, as they are not built to withstand pulling and tugging. Stuffed animals should be of the short-haired variety, and always check and make sure the hair won't shed.

6 TO 12 MONTHS

At this age your baby starts to become mobile, learning to roll over, sit up, crawl, stand, and eventually to walk. This means it is time to take your babyproofing precautions to a new level, moving any ob-ject you do not want your baby to put in her mouth someplace you are *sure* she cannot reach. Getting down on your hands and knees will make these hazards easier to spot.

You can no longer assume your baby will stay where you put him unless he is securely strapped in. Don't think your baby can't get to items that are just barely out of reach or across the room. New skills develop quickly—powered by insatiable curiosity.

What to do

- Now is the time to start using **baby gates** at the tops and bottoms of **stairs**, and to temporarily keep your child out of rooms where hazardous items (craft projects, older siblings' toys, etc.) are left unattended.
- Never leave your baby alone in the **bathroom**, or near any other container of water, such as a wading pool or bucket. Remove all

household toxic substances from the bathroom or kitchen, and all **medications** to a high shelf, or locked cabinet or room.

- Once your baby has reached at least twenty pounds, you can turn her safety seat around to face forward when riding in the **car**.
- Check your **child's bedroom**, your bedroom, **family room**, **bathroom**, etc. for small objects the baby might swallow, loose **electrical** cords or uncovered outlets, unstable furniture, sharp edges, etc.
- Always put your baby to sleep on his back, on a firm mattress, and avoid using too many blankets. This has been shown to reduce the risk of SIDS.
- The slats on your baby's crib should be no more than 2 3/8 inches apart, and it should meet all modern safety standards. Once your baby can stand up, remove bumper pads so she won't use them to climb out of the crib.
- Make sure your baby can't get into the diaper pail. This is a suffocation hazard, and the deodorizers found in many pails are toxic if swallowed.
- Make sure your baby's **clothing** has no drawstrings or other parts that could catch on a crib or doorknob. And watch for buttons, bows, or other decorations that could be pulled off and swallowed.
- When **diapering**, avoid using changing tables, opting instead for a changing pad in the crib or on the floor. Avoid hazardous products like baby powder.
- Secure **doors** that can pinch small fingers or let a child lock himself inside a room.
- Secure **electrical outlets/cords**, either with outlet covers and cord windup devices, or by moving heavy pieces of furniture in front of them.
- Keep **exercise equipment** out of sight, make sure all moving parts are covered, and install cord locks on electrical equipment so it can't be plugged in.
- Install the proper guards on your **fireplace**.

- Offer your child only **food** that is soft enough to chew, and is cut into pieces too small to get stuck in the throat. And make sure you prepare it safely. Food poisoning is quite serious in a child.
- Make sure your child's **high chair** has a sturdy base, and a safety strap to keep her seated. Never leave your child unattended in a high chair, and keep the chair away from hazardous objects on nearby tables or countertops.
- Never put your child in an **infant carrier seat** on any surface above floor level, and always strap him in.
- Take care when your baby is in the **kitchen**. It is best to use a high chair to keep him away from the stove and other hazardous objects.
- To avoid burns, never cook or carry hot food or drinks while holding your baby, and never set your coffee cup down within your child's reach.
- Periodically check your child's **pacifier** to make sure the nipple is in no danger of separating from the base and becoming stuck in the child's throat. Never tie a pacifier around your child's neck.
- Supervise your baby when playing with **pets**. Avoid reptiles as pets until your child is at least five years old.
- If you use a **playpen**, make sure the mesh holes are no larger than one-quarter inch, never leave the sides down when your baby is in the playpen, and never tie toys across the top of a playpen.
- Ride your child only in the seat of **shopping** carts, do not let her stand up, and never leave her unattended.
- Buy **strollers** that meet JPMA safety guidelines, and make sure your child is securely strapped in at all times.
- Limit your child's time in the **sun** during peak hours, and always make use of sunscreen and protective clothing when in the sun.
- Avoid baby **walkers**.
- Make sure all **windows**—especially above the first floor—are secured with bars or latches, and that all dangling window cords are kept out of your child's reach.

Toy Guidelines

At this age keep toys simple and sturdy, and don't give your child any toy you wouldn't want him to put in his mouth. Your child's playthings should be strong enough for him to stand on without breaking. Toys should be too large to get stuck in a child's windpipe, nostrils, or ears, and should contain no small parts that can detach or break off. There should be no part that can pinch small fingers, and the toy should be free of toxic materials or paints.

If your child is ready to enter the art world, make sure it is only with large-size, nontoxic crayons and large, sturdy sheets of paper. Take care, because even these large-size crayons can break into pieces your baby can swallow. Budding literati can feast on lightweight books (so she won't hurt herself) at least six to eight inches square, made of cloth, plastic, or heavy cardboard that is colorfast and nontoxic.

These pretoddlers can enjoy stacking blocks as small as two inches, but keep in mind that any toy that will fit through a cardboard toilet-paper tube will also fit into your child's windpipe, and is a choking hazard.

And it's time to take down that mobile, or move it well out of reach. These look-at toys are not constructed to withstand children of this age, and could break into small pieces that would present a choking hazard. Push-pull toys for your new walker should be at least five to seven inches in size, with large wheels and rollers. Puzzles should have no more than three pieces (too large to be swallowed), with rounded edges.

1 TO 2 YEARS

Between ages one and two, your baby will master the art of toddling, and then the art of walking steadily. She'll become increasingly independent and eager to explore things on her own. While learning to walk, she'll take a lot of falls, and is likely to trip over anything in her path (objects on the floor, a wrinkle in the carpet, etc.). Make sure she has plenty of clear walking space, and that sharp edges are kept well away from heavy traffic areas.

The fact that she can now stand and reach for things with both hands also means you have to take your babyproofing efforts to a new level. It's time to move dangerous or breakable objects even farther out of reach.

When your child begins to climb, you'll also have to keep dangerous things out of sight. Limit temptation (things your child may want to climb up to reach) and opportunity (pieces of furniture placed near things your child may want to reach) as much as possible. If you thought you had to keep an eye on her when she learned to crawl, you ain't seen nothin' yet.

What to do

- Choose only **art supplies** that are nontoxic and do not present a choking hazard if swallowed.
- **Baby gates** may still be useful in some situations, but don't rely on them to replace regular babyproofing.
- Never leave your baby alone in the **bathroom**, or near any other container of water, such as a wading pool or bucket. Remove all household toxic substances from the bathroom or kitchen, and all **medications** to a high shelf, or locked cabinet or room.
- Always use a **car** seat for your child, and put him in the backseat.
- In your **child's bedroom**, make sure that dressers and other furniture won't fall over if she climbs on them. Make sure toy chests with lids won't fall closed and injure or trap your child.
- Set your child's crib mattress at the lowest setting, and keep the crib free of toys and other objects he might stack up and use to climb out.

- Once your child can climb out of her crib, or when she is two years old, move her to a regular bed.
- Make sure your child wears sturdy, slip-proof shoes, and that his other **clothing** is free of drawstrings or other loose parts that might catch on playground equipment, etc.
- Secure **doors** to keep your child from pinching his fingers or locking himself in.
- Secure **electrical outlets/cords**, either with outlet covers and cord windup devices, or by moving heavy pieces of furniture in front of them.
- Keep **exercise equipment** out of sight, if possible, make sure all moving parts are covered, and install cord locks on electrical equipment so it can't be plugged in. This is especially important while your child is fond of imitating you.
- Check your child's bedroom, your bedroom, **family room**, **bathroom**, etc. for small objects the baby might swallow, unstable furniture, sharp edges etc.
- Install a proper guard on your **fireplace**, and keep matches and keys to gas jets out of sight.
- Offer your child only **food** that is cut into chokeproof pieces. And prepare your family's food carefully, to minimize the threat of food poisoning, which can be fatal in children of this age.
- Make sure your child's **high chair** has a stable base, and always strap him in.
- Take care when your child is in the **kitchen**. Putting him in a high chair or in an out-of-the-way corner and giving him some pots, pans, and spoons to play with may help keep him safely distracted.
- Always supervise children and **pets**. Avoid having reptiles as pets until your child is at least five years old.
- Make sure **playgrounds** your child uses, whether at home or the park, are filled with safe equipment that has protective surfacing underneath.
- Don't let your child stand in **shopping** carts. Take extra care to

keep your child from wandering away and getting into trouble if you are letting her walk.

- Hold your toddler's hand whenever you are near the **street**. This is a good time to start teaching traffic safety.
- Buy **strollers** that meet JPMA safety guidelines, and make sure your child is securely strapped in at all times.
- Keep your toddler out of the **sun** during peak hours, and protect him with a waterproof, nonirritating sunscreen and proper clothing and sunglasses when you go out.
- Monitor your child's **television** viewing. Make sure programs are age-appropriate.
- Make sure all **windows**—especially above the first floor—are secured with bars or latches, and that all dangling window cords are kept out of your child's reach.
- Supervise your toddler whenever she is playing in your **yard**, and if possible, keep her safe with a fence or other barrier.

Toy Guidelines

Even though your child may be more and more interested in drawing, it is still important to limit his art-supply choices to large, nontoxic crayons. After nineteen months or so, you can introduce paper books to your child's library (of course, any book is okay if the child is not playing with it unsupervised). Small, light wooden blocks can now be added to her cache of construction materials, as well as blocks as large as twelve inches in length for nineteen months and up. Dolls as small as five or six inches are now okay, but be on the lookout for dolls with parts smaller than two or three inches that can break off and be swallowed. If your child shows an interest in stringing beads, make sure the string is less than twelve inches long to prevent strangulation, and that you allow your child to play only with beads too large to be swallowed. Beads should be wood or plastic—never glass. Climbing platforms for this age group should be no more than twelve inches off the ground, and slides no higher than fifteen to twenty inches, all surrounded by the appropriate protective surfacing. (See "Playgrounds.") Play figures are not generally appropriate until nineteen months, when figures should be at least three to five inches tall and two inches wide. Push-pull toys for this age group should be broad-based with low centers of gravity to prevent flipping. Ride-on toys should also be well balanced, with large wheels. Child's toes should touch the floor when seated. The bases of rocking horses should extend in all directions for stability.

3 TO 5 YEARS

Your child is now becoming able to do more and more on her own. She walks and runs confidently, and can probably even show you some new tricks on the playground climbing structure. But her motor skills are still way ahead of her judgment, so you need to keep a close eye on her.

Though she may want to run ahead of you when you are out for a walk, you need to keep a firm grip on her hand, because she is likely to forget that there are cars in the street and dart out into traffic. Though she can easily climb to the top of the monkey bars, she might not realize that they are too high for her to jump down safely.

She's also not beyond putting small objects absentmindedly into her mouth, which means you still need to watch out for choking hazards—especially things like broken balloons, coins, or small toys.

What to do

- Take care to choose **art supplies** that are nontoxic. Children this age should use only plastic safety scissors for cutting.
- Since your child will now be using the **bathroom** alone, you need to be especially careful to pick up things like **medicines**,

razors, mouthwash, and other grown-up grooming aids. Even if she knows better than to touch these things, her desire to imitate you may get her in trouble. Also make sure she knows which faucet is the cold water, and which is hot, and adjust your hot-water heater to avoid scald burns.

- As soon as your child begins to ride a **bicycle**, he needs a properly fitting helmet and some clear lessons in the rules of the road. Children this age shouldn't ride without supervision, and should never ride in the street.
- Once your child reaches age four and weighs forty pounds, she is no longer legally required to ride in a **car seat**. However, the seat belt may still not fit well enough to protect her. Use a belt-positioning booster seat until it does.
- If your **child's bedroom** is home to a bunk bed, make sure it is sturdy, with no more than three inches of space between the headboard and the frame of the bed.
- Watch out for toy chests with lids that might fall closed and injure or trap your child.
- Have the proper guard on your **fireplace**, and keep matches and the key to gas jets out of sight and out of reach.
- Take care when preparing your child's **food**. Choking is still a hazard at this age, and food poisoning can be fatal to a young child.
- Keep toxic chemicals like cleaners, fertilizers, and gasoline, and all tools out of reach of children in the **garage**. Never store old refrigerators or freezers where children might be tempted to play inside them.
- Do not keep **guns** in your home. Children as young as three have the strength to pull the trigger.
- Take care when your child is in the **kitchen** with you. If he is interested in cooking, find safe tasks that will keep him busy and out from underfoot. Continue to store sharp objects, breakables, and cleaners well out of reach.
- Watch out for toys that make so much **noise** they could damage your child's hearing.

- Keep **plants** out of reach unless you are sure they aren't toxic.
- Know the **playgrounds** your child frequents, and make sure they contain safe equipment and proper protective surfacing.
- When your child is ready to start **school**, check out the grounds to make sure it is run safely. If you find hazards, get involved and get them fixed. Children this age are too young to walk to school, so make sure they know how to ride the bus safely, or make sure you know that whoever is giving them a ride is a safe driver.
- Never let your child stand up in a **shopping** cart. Teach her what to do if you become separated in a store or the mall.
- If your child is participating in **sports**, get to know the coach, find out what safety equipment is required, and get your child a preseason physical.
- Teach your child never to get into a car or go anywhere with **strangers**—someone they do not know. Teach them to scream "This is not my mom or dad" if they are being taken away by someone they don't know.
- Your child is still too young to cross the **street** alone, but make sure you are setting a good example every time you cross with her.
- Protect your child's skin from **sun** damage by using sunscreen, sunglasses, and proper clothing.
- Monitor your child's **television** viewing. Teach him to be a smart media consumer and not to settle for programs with gratuitous violence and little worthwhile content.
- Continue to use **window** guards—especially for windows above the first floor—and keep window cords out of your child's reach.
- Have a fenced **yard** or provide adequate supervision and clear boundaries to limit your child to a safe area.

Toy Guidelines

Children this age can begin to work with paint, clay, and markers— as long as these items are nontoxic—and can even use blunt-end scissors. Buy the plastic kind that cut paper, but not skin or hair.

Dolls for children this age can begin to have simple accessories, but make sure your child isn't inclined to put them in his mouth. Your child may begin to play her first board games, but make sure the pieces are at least two to four inches in size. Avoid games with dice until about age five. Your child may now be ready for the climbing equipment at the playground, but check it out thoroughly first for safety. (See "Playgrounds.") Your child may also be ready for her first tricycle. You'll want thirteen-inch wheels for ages three to four. Sandbox toys should still be kept simple, with no metal parts.

6 TO 8 YEARS

Your child will now be so independent that you may think he can take care of himself (he certainly thinks so!). But his judgment isn't really good enough to know what's safe and what isn't. He can certainly understand warnings like "Don't take any medicine unless Mommy gives it to you," but that may not stop him from chewing up a whole bottle of children's vitamins, which don't taste like medicine.

If your child is closer to seven or eight, she may feel you are treating her like a baby if you don't, for instance, let her cross the street by herself. But don't relax the rules just yet. Make her prove she can be trusted to make safe choices before letting her strike out on her own.

What to do

- Choose **art supplies** with care. Avoid items with toxic ingredients.
- Remove cleaners, **medicines**, and other hazards from the **bathroom**.

- Keep your child's **bicycle** in good repair, and make sure she knows the rules of the road. Set clear boundaries about where it is safe to ride, don't let her ride in the street or at night, and make sure she wears a helmet.
- Use a belt-positioning booster seat in the **car** until the seat belt fits correctly. Always make sure your child rides buckled up in the backseat.
- Watch for loose **clothing** or drawstrings that might catch on playground equipment, escalators, or school-bus doors.
- If you have a **computer**, keep track of the games your child is playing, the Web sites he is visiting, and anyone he has been in contact with on-line. This will be easier if the computer is in the living room rather than your child's bedroom.
- Teach your child about the hazards of putting objects into **electrical outlets**, and show her how to properly unplug electrical cords by grasping the plug.
- Keep tools and other hazardous objects out of reach in the **garage**.
- Do not store **guns** in your home.
- Take care when working with your child in the **kitchen**. Kids this age shouldn't be using appliances without supervision, and shouldn't be taking foods in or out of the oven or microwave.
- Watch out for cap guns and other toys that make enough noise to damage your child's hearing.
- Supervise your children when playing with **pets**.
- Reinforce the idea of using **playground** equipment properly, and make sure your child's playground has safe equipment and proper protective surfacing.
- Take a walk through your child's **school** to make sure the grounds feel safe to you. Inquire about tests for environmental hazards and policies regarding campus violence.
- If your child is participating in **sports**, make sure she is using the proper protective gear. Check out the coach to be sure proper safety practices are being taught.

- Teach your child common tricks **strangers** might use to try to lure him into an unsafe situation. Teach him to trust his instincts, and that it is okay to say no to an adult who wants to make him do something he is uncomfortable with.
- Your child is almost old enough to cross the **street** alone, so make sure he knows how to cross safely. Set a good example by *never* crossing unsafely when you are with your child.
- Make sure your child uses sunscreen and wears protective clothing out in the **sun**.
- Teach your child to choose only quality **television** programs that have good content and little violence.

Toy Guidelines

It is tempting at this age to buy your child toys meant for older children—especially if these are the toys he's asking for. But be careful about this. It is important to check out the toy carefully and make sure your child is really ready for it.

This is an age where children are especially interested in hobby and craft kits. You should choose these carefully, because some require the use of toxic glues or chemicals that could hurt your child if they come into contact with his skin. They also may use hot glue guns or other plug-in tools that are dangerous to your child.

"Combat toys" such as water and dart guns, slingshots, boomerangs, etc. also are a big hit with the six-to-eight set. Some of these projectile-launching toys can cause eye injuries, and the rough-and-tumble play that goes with them causes still more. Make sure the toy guns, etc., your child chooses do not use ammunition that could cause injury, and make sure he is playing in a safe, open area where he is less likely to get hurt.

9 TO 12 YEARS

At this age, your child will be spending more and more time outside your supervision—at after-school activities and sports practice, visiting friends in the neighborhood, riding her bike, etc. So you'll have to rely on her sound judgment to keep her safe.

By teaching your child safe habits, such as looking carefully before crossing the street, staying alert and wearing a helmet when riding a bike, and always wearing a seat belt in the car, you've set the stage for her to stay safe on her own. This doesn't mean she no longer needs your supervision or advice, and you should take advantage of these opportunities to reinforce her good judgment for times when you're not around.

What to do

- Avoid **art supplies** with toxic ingredients, and hobby kits that make use of electricity or sharp tools—unless you are there to supervise. Take special care when choosing supplies meant for professionals.
- Children under ten should never ride **bicycles** in the street or at night. Whatever her age, make sure your child always wears a helmet and knows how to ride safely.
- When riding in the **car**, make sure your child is always buckled up, with the shoulder belt across the shoulder and chest and the lap belt low and tight around the hips.
- Make sure your child's **clothing** doesn't have drawstrings, or fit so loosely it could get caught in playground equipment or school-bus doors.
- Know your child's **computer**. Familiarize yourself with her favorite games and sites, and watch out for violent or sexual content. Also keep tabs on your child's on-line correspondence and teach her never to give out personal information via the Internet.

- Do not store **guns** in your home.
- Supervise your child in the **kitchen**. No one under age eight or ten should take food in or out of the oven, food processor, or blender.
- Watch out for stereos, headphones, and other loud **noise** that could damage your child's hearing. If you can hear the music coming from your child's headphones when he is walking by, it's too loud.
- Teach your child to treat **pets** with care and respect. An animal that is chased or teased is more likely to bite or scratch.
- Check out any **playgrounds** your child frequents. Look for a safe atmosphere and safe equipment.
- Take a walk around your child's **school** to make sure the grounds seem safe. Ask your principal about testing for environmental hazards.
- If your child plays **sports**, get to know the coach. Make sure he or she is requiring the proper safety equipment and reinforcing the rules of safe participation.
- Teach your child common tricks **strangers** might use to try to lure him into an unsafe situation. Teach him to trust his instincts, and that it is okay to say no to an adult who wants to make him do something he is uncomfortable with.
- Make sure your child always crosses the **street** safely.
- Teach your child to use sunscreen before going out in the **sun**.
- Limit **television** viewing, and help your child select only quality shows with good content and little violence.

Toy Guidelines

There aren't many toys that are dangerous to your child at this age— if they are used properly. At this age, it is more likely to be the child's imagination than the toy itself that creates a hazard. Watch out for children who like to take toys apart—especially electronic toys.

You should also be there to supervise the use of modeling kits, chemistry sets, and other toys that might contain toxic glues or chemicals. You should also beware "toys" like BB guns, air rifles, and fireworks, which could seriously injure or even kill your child.

Section II

A-TO-Z GUIDE TO CHILD SAFETY

AIR TRAVEL

"Welcome aboard, and thank you for flying with us today." That's probably about as much of the preflight safety lecture as you pay attention to these days. Not a very good example if you are flying with kids.

In fact, if your children are old enough, you should translate the "please take a moment to locate the exit nearest you" and other safety stuff for their benefit. "I think it's helpful for the parent to put it in terms that children can understand, but not to the point of frightening the child," says Jill Gallagher of the Association of Flight Attendants.

Before the flight

If your little aviator is only old enough to remember one or two important points, show him where the nearest exit is, says Gallagher, and tell him that if there is an emergency, he should listen to the flight attendant. At the start of the flight, introduce your child to the flight attendant so he will know who is in charge and where to go for help. This also alerts the flight attendant that there is a small child on the plane who may need assistance, says Gallagher. Remember that if there is an emergency, you may not be able to help your child make it to safety.

Please remain seated

Although most airlines let children under age two ride on their parents' laps free of charge, the Association of Flight Attendants recommends buying your child a ticket so she can ride in an infant seat. The safety seat should not be more than sixteen inches wide, to fit between the airplane seat's armrests.

If you choose not to bring an infant seat, you should still tell the airline you will be traveling with a baby so there will be an extra oxygen mask available. If your child is riding on your lap, do not fasten the seat belt around both of you. If there is an impact, your weight could crush her between you and the seat belt.

The Federal Aviation Administration joins the AFA in recommending safety seats for infants and children small enough to fit into standard child safety seats, but does not allow booster seats for toddlers. In test results released in September 1994, the FAA reported that rear-facing carriers were a definite safety benefit for children weighing less than twenty pounds, and that forward-facing carriers—while they did not provide the same level of protection they would if installed in a car—do provide protection not afforded by normal lap belts.

Booster seats, however, bring children too close to the seat back in front of them, allowing their heads to be thrown against the rigid seat. Likewise, harness systems actually give less protection than the plane's own lap belt. The harnesses tested did not work properly with the plane's seat belt, and allowed test dummies to be thrown from their seats.

The FAA concluded that children too large to fit into standard safety seats were safer wearing only the plane's lap belt.

Ear, ear!

If your child has an ear infection, allergies, or a bad cold, it may not be a good idea to fly at all, according to Robert Ruder, M.D., who chairs the department of head and neck surgery/otolaryngology at Cedars Sinai Medical Center and is assistant clinical professor of head and neck surgery at UCLA Medical Center. Because congestion blocks the passages that would normally allow ear fluid to drain, you risk bursting the eardrum if you expose the ear to the increased pressure from takeoff and landing. "It's like putting a balloon over a water faucet," explains Ruder. "It keeps filling and filling and eventually it explodes."

Ruder strongly recommends against taking on an airplane a child with a bad case of congestion. But if you have no choice, he offers a few suggestions to lessen the risk of permanent damage and make the flight more comfortable.

An hour before takeoff, give your child a dose of Sudafed or another over-the-counter decongestant, and a dose of decongestant nasal spray. Then, during takeoff and landing, have your child close his mouth and blow while you hold his nose, to equalize the pressure between the inner and outer ear. "Make a game of it and have them pretend they are blowing up a balloon," suggests Ruder, "because if you just tell them to hold their nose and blow, they won't do it."

This same treatment (minus the balloon trick) will work for infants and toddlers, but check with your pediatrician first.

Flying solo

Children as young as five are allowed to fly alone, but I don't know many five-year-olds I would put on a plane by themselves (certainly no child of mine!). Ages five to seven can solo on flights that require no change of planes, and kids eight to eleven can fly alone even with a change of planes. Anyone over age twelve is considered an adult and can take any flight unassisted.

As a parent, you are the best judge of whether your child is ready for this experience. Be sure to prepare children of any age, explaining to them what the flight will be like, how long it will take, and what will happen while they are on the plane. Make sure your child knows he must obey the flight attendant's instructions, and make a backup plan in case something goes wrong. Give your child a phone number to call for help, and teach him to call collect.

In the airport

In a large crowd where your attention is focused elsewhere, it is easy to lose track of your most important piece of cargo. Be prepared for this frightening possibility.

- Teach your child to find a *uniformed* airline employee if he becomes lost. A long wait at the gate or ticket counter is a good time to make a game of spotting uniforms.
- Even children who would normally be able to recite their name and the names of their parents may clam up when lost and frightened. Hang a luggage tag marked with all the pertinent information, including your flight number, on your child to help those trying to help her. Attaching a picture of yourself means you can be identified quickly as your child's parent.
- Carry a current picture of your child, with height, weight, and other vital statistics written on the back. This information is important, and easily forgotten in an emergency.
- Teach your child what to do if approached by a stranger. (See also "Strangers.")

A little preflight preparation is the key to having a safe trip, and getting the whole family ready for takeoff.

Resources

"Kids in Flight," from the Association of Flight Attendants; (202) 328-5400.
"Toddlers Not Protected by Airline Safety Seats," *Your Child's Wellness Newsletter,* September/October 1995, p. 2.
"The Performance of Child Restraint Devices in Transport Airplane Passenger Seats," a Report from the Office of Aviation Medicine of the Fed-

eral Aviation Administration. Available through the National Technical Information Service, Springfield, VA 22161.

ART SUPPLIES

Color, cut, paint, and paste—these things are such a natural part of childhood that it's hard to imagine them as unsafe. But they can be if you don't choose your child's art materials with care. Many of these products contain hazardous ingredients, and it is only by reading the label that you can tell them from their safe counterparts.

Glue

Many glues and adhesives contain solvents, which give off toxic vapors. They produce a narcotic effect when inhaled (kids even sniff them to get high) and are highly flammable. According to the Washington Toxics Coalition, the most dangerous of these include contact cement, epoxy, instant glues, plastic adhesives, and model glues. But the nastiest by far is rubber cement, which contains hexane or heptane—nervous-system depressants that can cause permanent nerve dammage. Use a glue stick, paste, or white glue instead.

Paint

Oil-based paints contain volatile solvents that dissolve the pigment and allow the paint to spread. But even the safer water-based paints can contain toxic pigments such as arsenic, cadmium, or lead. Artists' paints, which are exempt from hazard labeling laws, fail to warn consumers about these ingredients and should never be given to children. Children should also not use powdered paints, which produce hazardous dust when they are mixed. Liquid, water-based formulas are generally safest.

Pens and markers

There are three types of markers: aromatic solvent-based (most toxic because they contain xylene), alcohol-based (containing alcohol, a less toxic solvent than xylene), and water-based (the safest, and the ones your child should use).

Any pen labeled "permanent" is likely xylene or alcohol-based, as is any pen with a distinct odor. Dry-erase markers are all solvent-based, and shouldn't be used by children.

Felt-tip markers scented with fruit flavors are not necessarily toxic, but will get your child in the unhealthy habit of sniffing markers or putting them in their mouths.

Scissors

Until your child has learned proper scissor etiquette (yes, don't run with them) and is coordinated enough to cut only what he intends to cut, I recommend allowing only plastic safety scissors within reach. These amazing little tools cut paper rather nicely, but won't cut skin, fabric, or hair. (I can vouch for this. My daughter tried it all.)

It is still a good idea to treat these as if they were "real" scissors so that your child can learn the proper way to handle the sharp variety. Make your child ask permission before cutting with the scissors, show her how to keep her fingers, etc. out of the way when cutting, and teach her to hold them "point down" when walking.

On the label

The law requires that art supplies containing toxic or hazardous materials carry a warning label, and since products usually carry the least severe warning required, you should take these warnings *very* seriously:

- *Poison* means as little as a taste could be fatal.
- *Danger* means the product is toxic, flammable, or corrosive, and will burn eyes and skin on contact.
- *Warning* or *Caution* signifies a lesser hazard usually explained by a short statement such as "harmful if swallowed," or "avoid skin contact."

And even if you flunked chemistry, you can check labels for highly toxic ingredients, such as those on this Washington Toxics Coalition list:

acid and bases (concentrated)
cadmium
chromium (or chrome)
formaldehyde
hexane
lead
mercury
methyl alcohol (methanol)
methylene chloride
phenol
styrene
trichloroethane
trichloroethylene
toluene
turpentine
xylene

The label may also contain information from the Arts and Creative Materials Institute, a nonprofit organization of art-materials manufacturers that sponsors a certification program for children's art materials. Any product that bears one of their nontoxic labels has been tested by their toxicology experts and deemed safe for children.

For their list of certified materials, write to the Arts & Creative Materials Institute, 100 Boylston St., Suite 1050, Boston, MA 02116.

Though their certified materials are completely safe for children, ACMI recommends teaching your children good safety habits— such as never putting art materials, their pens, or brushes into their mouths.

Do it yourself

If you're still going crazy trying to remember which ingredients are bad and which are worse, try the sane approach and make your kids' art supplies (or let them do it) from the safe foodstuffs in your kitchen.

Resources

"Art and Hobby Supplies," from the Washington Toxics Coalition; (206) 632-1545.

"What You Need to Know About the Safety of Art & Craft Materials," from the Arts & Creative Materials Institute, Inc.; (617) 426-6400.

"Law Requires Review and Labeling of Art Materials Including Children's Art and Drawing Products," from the U.S. Consumer Product Safety Commission; (301) 504-0400.

ASBESTOS

There was a time when products such as insulation, ironing-board covers, and even oven mitts boasted of their asbestos content—but not anymore. Now that the mere mention of the material strikes fear into the hearts of home owners, few products are made with it. But that doesn't mean it's not around.

Your home probably contains asbestos if it was built anytime before the late 1970s, when the government cracked down and banned the stuff. It is most likely to show up:

- On roofing and siding shingles.
- In the insulation of houses built between 1930 and 1950.
- In textured paint and patching compounds put on before 1977.
- In artificial ashes and embers contained in gas-fired fireplaces.
- In walls and floors around wood-burning stoves.
- In vinyl floor tiles, and the adhesives that hold them in place.
- Around hot-water and steam pipes.
- In the insulation of oil and coal furnaces.

High-level exposure to asbestos can lead to increased risk of lung cancer, cancer of the chest lining and abdominal cavity, and scarring of the lungs. Symptoms, however, do not usually appear for twenty to thirty years after initial exposure, so protecting against asbestos is a long-term investment.

Leave well enough alone

Your first order of business if you suspect or discover there is asbestos in your house is not to panic. Don't grab the yellow pages and start calling abatement contractors (you may spend big money needlessly), and don't try to vanquish this hazard yourself (you may make the problem worse). Just stand back, take a deep breath well away from the stuff in question, and assess the situation.

- If the material is in good condition, and not showing any signs of wear and tear, limit access to the area and leave it alone. Asbestos isn't dangerous unless it is releasing fibers into the air. Having it removed, or even having it sampled to see if it is, indeed, asbestos, may create a hazard where none existed. Just inspect the material regularly, looking for tears, abrasions, or water damage. Avoid dusting, sweeping, sawing, sanding, or scraping the stuff—or doing anything else that might damage it.

- If the material is crumbling or damaged, or you are planning a remodeling project that would disturb the material, get in touch with a consultant who can determine if it contains asbestos. Asbestos can only be identified through a special microscope, and sampling should be done by a trained professional. The EPA should be able to refer you to a licensed contractor. Also keep in mind that you should never hire the same person to assess a problem *and* fix it. Never hire an inspector affiliated with an asbestos-correction firm.

- If you have damaged asbestos material in your home, having it repaired so it can't release dangerous fibers should be the first option you investigate. This is usually done either by sealing or covering the area in question, and should always be done by a professional. This person should work with the material only when wet, and should take special measures to contain and clean up dust. Again, the EPA should be able to help you find someone qualified.

- If the material is too badly damaged, or if you plan to remodel that part of your home, removal may be your only option. But make sure you investigate all other possibilities first. Asbestos abatement is extremely expensive, and can actually make conditions in your home worse if done improperly.

Resources

"Asbestos: Try Not to Panic," *Consumer Reports,* July 1995, pp. 468–469. For reprints of this report, write to CU/Reprints, 101 Truman Ave., Yonkers, N.Y. 10703-1057.

Asbestos in Your Home, from the American Lung Association, the Consumer Product Safety Commission ([800] 638-CPSC) and the Environ-mental Protection Agency ([202] 554-1404).

BABY GATES/ENCLOSURES

If you have stairs, baby gates are an essential, and they can also be helpful if you need to keep a child out of a room temporarily (I rec-ommend babyproofing every room in your home so that you don't have to keep the kids out of a room on a permanent basis). And it's essential to choose the right gate and use it safely.

The gatekeeper

You'll go a long way toward avoiding accidents and unauthorized fence scaling if you use this equipment as an extra measure of safety—not as a babysitter. You should supervise your baby at all times, and not leave him alone behind a gate. If you must be out of the room, use a baby monitor and check frequently (every few minutes) to make sure everything is okay.

The safest type of gate is one with a straight top edge and rigid mesh screen. Babies have been strangled when they caught their heads in the V-shaped openings along the top of accordion-style gates and enclosures.

Anchor the gate securely to the doorway it is blocking—espe-cially if it is at the top of a staircase. A child who pushes the gate over could fall all the way down the stairs.

If your gate uses an expanding pressure bar to hold it in place, put the bar on the side that's away from your child. These bars make a handy foothold she could use to scale the fence (and the landing might be a rough one).

And while you're using a gate to block off a room or stairway, remember that you have to close it *every single time you go through* for it to provide any measure of protection.

Enclosures

I don't recommend using expandable enclosures on a regular basis, but they may provide the safest temporary solution when you must leave your baby unsupervised for a few minutes, or if you are visiting a house that is not childproofed. You should never leave your baby unsupervised there for long, even when she is sleeping.

Never use or purchase an accordion-style expandable enclosure. They pose the same hazards as accordion-style baby gates, and could trap your child's head and strangle him.

Overall, thorough childproofing is preferable to baby gates and enclosures (except in the case of stairways) because eventually, someone will leave the gate open or forget that the baby is not inside the enclosure. If you haven't childproofed the room, the baby is then vulnerable to whatever hazards are left unchecked. Save these devices as a backup plan for times when you have to leave hazards temporarily in the child's path (e.g., a sewing or hobby project is spread out all over the floor, there are too many people in the kitchen for you to really watch the baby).

Resources

"Safe and Sound for Baby: A Guide to Baby-Product Safety, Use and Selection," from the Juvenile Products Manufacturers Association, 2 Greentree Centre, Box 955, Marlton, NJ 08053.

The Safe Nursery: A Booklet to Help Avoid Injuries from Nursery Furniture and Equipment and "Tips for Your Baby's Safety," from the U.S. Consumer Product Safety Commission; (800) 638-2772.

BABYSITTERS

"But what will we do with the kids?"

You want them to be safe. You want them well cared for. But you also want to get out of the house and see that movie, eat at that restaurant, hike that mountain trail. . . .

So where do you find a good, safe, reliable, dependable babysitter? First look for a willing, teenage-type person. Next, determine if that person is responsible and has the necessary skills.

What your sitter should know

Basic first aid and CPR are skills your sitter *must* have. A nationwide program called Safe Sitter has been teaching these lifesaving talents, along with a healthy dose of child-care basics, since 1980. Their courses are offered at hospitals and other facilities nationwide, and include most of the babysitting basics covered in this chapter. To find out if there is a program near you, you can write to Safe Sitter National Headquarters, 1500 North Ritter Ave., Indianapolis, IN. Their toll-free number is (800) 255-4089.

In the event there isn't a Safe Sitter program in your neck of the woods, contact your local Red Cross, which will at least offer CPR and first-aid courses. These programs will teach your sitter to respond to all emergency situations, including illness, injuries, accidental poisonings, and natural disasters.

To avoid using these emergency skills, your sitter should be able to identify run-of-the-mill household dangers (the stairs, the pool, storage areas, the medicine cabinet) and know enough to keep your children away from them. Of course, the better the job you've done making your home safe for your kids, the fewer the dangers your sitter will have to worry about. Then all *you* will have to worry about is that the sitter keeps your safeguards in place (i.e., remembers to relatch the baby gate over the stairs, puts household cleaners back out of reach after cleaning up messes).

Your sitter should be responsible enough to provide constant supervision for an infant, and to know where older children are and what they are up to at all times. She should have a sense of what toys are appropriate for children of various ages, and what items are unsafe—especially if you have a baby or toddler who could choke on small objects left within reach.

If you have a baby, your sitter should know how to change the baby safely. (See "Diapering.") Show your sitter where all the "changing stuff" is kept and put it within reach so he doesn't have to leave the baby unattended to search for a needed item.

If your sitter will be feeding your baby or toddler and you use a high chair, remind her to strap the baby in. Show her how the straps work, and make sure she can fasten them correctly. Prepare the food or bottles yourself in advance (so table food can be cut in pieces small enough that your child won't choke), and give specific, written instructions about how to heat it up. If you allow the sitter to use the microwave, make sure she stirs the food thoroughly before feeding to avoid hot spots. It never hurts to prepare a little something for the sitter to eat as well. They get hungry, too.

The sitter should also know how to put your baby to sleep safely, on his side on a firm mattress—never on a blanket or quilt.

Your sitter should always keep doors and windows locked, and should never open the door to strangers. If he thinks there is reason to be concerned, he should contact you immediately. He should also screen telephone calls using your answering machine. If it's you, he can pick up. If it's someone else, let them leave a message. Under no circumstances should your sitter say "this is the babysitter," or give any indication that you are not at home.

If your sitter is taking your child out of the house, to a park or playground, she should know how to properly supervise them on the equipment. (See "Playgrounds.") It may help to fill her in on your child's skill level (e.g., Suzy can go down the slide all by herself, or Todd only uses the infant swing).

Above all, *your sitter must know how to control your kids*. If they won't follow her instructions, she can't keep them safe. Go over your discipline policies (the ones that work) in front of the children so that they know the sitter is in charge and are sure what they can expect if they get out of line. Of course you should make it clear that the sitter is never to hit the kids (nor should the kids hit the sitter). The sitter should also be able to win your kids' trust so that they will listen to her even in an emergency situation where they are frightened.

Another thing your sitter should have are personal references. You should be able to talk to parents he has sat for, as well as the children themselves, if they're old enough. Find out how the parents and the kids feel about the sitter, and be sure to inquire if he has had to handle any emergency situations. A sitter with experience caring for children the same ages as yours is great, but not essential.

At some point, no matter what evidence your prospective sitter has presented in his or her favor, you're going to have to go with your gut. Does this person look and act like a responsible individual who will take good care of your children? Do you feel comfortable leaving them in this person's care? Do your children feel comfortable with this person? (Yes, they should be present at the interview. The best sitter in the world won't do you any good if the kids are terrified of her and won't let you leave the house.)

And don't just pick one sitter. Pick at least two, if you can find them, so you aren't caught using an untested sitter if your regular sitter is unavailable. Alternate between sitters so your children are familiar with both.

Preparing for departure

So you've found your safe sitter, he's free Friday night, and you're getting ready to go. But your work isn't finished yet. You not only have to get ready to go out, you have to get ready for the sitter.

First, call a *nearby* adult friend or relative (this has to be some-one over age eighteen who can drive and can take legal responsi-bility for your children, if necessary) who will be home during the time you are out, and will be reachable in an emergency. This should be someone you trust to handle trouble.

Next, take a large envelope, write an emergency medical release in that person's name, and seal it inside, along with your child's in-surance card. On the outside of the envelope, write your emer-gency information:

- The telephone number and address of the place you will be, as well as your cellular phone or beeper number, if applicable.
- The name, address, and telephone number of your backup adult.
- The name, address, and telephone number of your child's doctor, as well as the address of the nearest emergency facility or urgent-care center (important if you have an HMO).
- Your child's full name, your full name, and your home address, with clear directions to your house. (This is important if some-one has to call 911. Your sitter may not know your address, or may forget it in an emergency.)
- List anything your child is allergic to, or any medical conditions (e.g., asthma).

Tape this envelope to the telephone, and instruct the sitter to take it with her if she needs to take your child to a doctor or to call an ambulance. If there is an emergency, the sitter should call your backup adult and 911, then you.

Post it

Your next job is to take a tour of your house, with Post-it pad and pen in hand. Hunt down all the hazards, and mark them accord-ingly. "Keep this cabinet locked at all times" is probably appropri-ate for the cupboard where you store your cleaning products, while "the kids are not allowed to play in here" will serve you well taped to your office or workshop door.

Sitter's here

Safe Sitter recommends allowing thirty to forty-five minutes before you must leave the house to acclimate a new sitter and let the kids warm up to her. (Subsequent visits by the same sitter will require less time, but you should still allow at least fifteen to twenty minutes.)

When the sitter arrives, point out the emergency envelope you've created, then give him a tour of the Post-it notes and any other hazards you can think of that you haven't been able to completely kid-proof.

Point out the locations of things the sitter will probably need, such as the kids' clothes and toys, the food you've prepared for dinner, etc.

Next point out your first-aid stuff (Band-Aids, antiseptic, syrup of ipecac) and your emergency supplies and emergency exits, flashlights, fire and burglar alarms (see "Disasters"), and explain your family's disaster plan (how you plan to keep everyone safe during a natural disaster). Always have a first-aid chart within easy reach. (You can get one by calling the American Academy of Pediatrics at [800] 433-9016).

Now give your sitter a safe place to store her purse, backpack, or anything else she brought with her. This should be somewhere easily accessible to her, but not to the kids. (You don't know what might be in your sitter's luggage, and you don't want to offend him or her by searching it.)

You should also discuss the kids' routines—feeding, nap/bed times, snacking, how you want the baby picked up and whether the sitter should pick her up every time she cries, your kids' comfort toys and personality quirks. And go over house rules—how much television and phone time is allowed, whether the kids can have visitors. Make it clear that smoking and alcohol are not allowed in your house. Also make it clear that the sitter is not allowed visitors, since they are almost guaranteed to distract her from supervising your kids.

Things you should know enough not to ask of your sitter

- Don't ask her to bathe your baby. If you haven't had time to do it yourself, maybe baby can skip his bath today. It's simply too dangerous—especially if your sitter doesn't have much experience with babies.
- Don't ask him to take your kids swimming. Unless this sitter is a Red Cross–certified lifeguard, it's not worth the risk. Children in the pool require adult supervision at all times.
- Don't ask her to give your child medication. If your child is ill and needs medicine, or is finishing up a course of antibiotics, give it yourself before you leave—or stay home and go out when your child is well. If you must leave a sick child, it is better to leave her with an adult relative, if one is available.
- Don't ask your sitter to try to control a child you can't control yourself. If your kids won't listen, your sitter can't stop unsafe behavior.
- Don't ask your sitter to do a lot of routine household tasks (cooking, cleaning, laundry) that will take her time and attention away from the children.

Questions to ask your child the next day

You can determine a lot about how responsible your sitter is by asking the kids how they spent their time while you were away. You don't have to grill them, just ask casually, and pay close attention to their answers. What games did their sitter play with them? What did they watch on television? Did anything happen that made them feel uncomfortable? What did they eat? You get the idea.

Note: For this strategy to work, your kids must be able to speak without fear of punishment. If they get in trouble because they tell you they watched a TV show you don't normally allow, or had ice cream for dinner, they'll never let you in on what's happening again.

Resources

"Ten Tips for Safe Sitting" and "What Your Babysitter Needs to Know," from Safe Sitter; (800) 255-4089.

"The Super Sitter," Document #4243 from the U.S. Consumer Product Safety Commission; (800) 638-2772.

"Parental Guidelines in Case You Need a Babysitter," from the National Center for Missing and Exploited Children; (703) 235-3900.

BATHROOM

Don't let that gleaming tile fool you. This tiny room is an accident waiting to happen.

- Scald/burn hazards—the bathtub, sink, and shower.
- Poisoning potential—the medicine cabinet, cleaners, mouthwash.
- Drowning danger—the tub and toilet.
- Slip-and-fall possibilities—the bathtub, wet floors, unsecured rugs.
- Electrocution hazards—small appliances (blow dryers, curling irons, electric razors).

Hotter water

Nearly thirty-five thousand children are treated in emergency rooms for scald burns each year. When you think of a child being burned, the bathtub isn't the first thing that comes to mind, but injuries are more severe and deaths more common from bathtub scalds than from scalds caused by spills in the kitchen, and the average bathtub scalding accident covers 12 percent of the body with a third-degree burn, according to the Gas Appliance Manufacturers' Association and the National Safe Kids Campaign.

The first thing you should do to protect your child from scalds in the bathroom—and the rest of your house—is to turn your water heater down to 120 degrees Fahrenheit.

Most home water heaters are set at 155 degrees, according to the Alisa Ann Ruch Burn Foundation, and at this temperature it takes just *one second* to give a child a second- or third-degree burn. Turning your water heater down to 120 degrees buys your child a full five minutes before a serious burn takes place. Comfortable tub temperature, by the way, is about 100 degrees.

Fill up the tub and turn off the water (hot first) before you put your child in, and remember *your hand goes into the water before your child*. Even if you checked the water temperature while the tub was filling, check it again. Run your hand through the whole tub to check for hot spots. And, of course, never leave your child unattended in the bathtub. He could turn on the hot water and burn himself.

If your child is old enough to use the bathroom alone, tie a red ribbon on the sink's hot-water faucet to help her remember which one it is.

Drowning prevention

Pools aren't the only places where kids drown. In fact, children under age one most frequently drown in bathtubs or buckets, and nearly 8 percent of all childhood drownings occur in bathtubs, according to the National Safe Kids Campaign. It takes as little as an inch of water and three to five minutes for a child to drown, so again, never leave your baby or toddler alone in the tub—no matter how little water is in it. And don't rely on bath seats or rings to keep your child safe. The Consumer Product Safety Commission reports that children have drowned when their seats tipped over, when they slipped between the legs of the seat and became trapped underwater, or when they climbed out of the seat.

The only guaranteed way to prevent bathtub drowning is to stay with your child. If you are alone in your home and bathing your baby or toddler, lock your doors and do not answer them unless you take the baby with you. If the phone rings—well, that's what answering machines are for. At least eighty children a year drown in bathtubs. Don't let one of this year's casualties be yours.

Toilet drownings are another hazard. If a baby or toddler topples headfirst into the toilet, he probably won't be able to get out. Toilet locks, available at hardware stores and babyproofing outlets, will help keep your baby out of the toilet. But simply keeping the lid closed is often enough to keep kids out.

A slick trick

A fall in the bathroom is especially dangerous because it's a mine-field of chrome and porcelain. Nonskid mats in the tub and on the bathroom floor will help prevent these falls. Watch out for residue from bath oils, which can make even rubber mats slick. Always rinse the tub thoroughly after using one of these products. An inflatable plastic guard or towel placed over your bath fixtures when your child is in the tub is also certain to save him a nasty bruise or two.

There she blows

Each year, seventeen people are electrocuted when their blow dry-ers fall into water, estimates the CPSC. Ten of these are children under age ten.

To protect your whole family against electrocution or electric shock from small appliances in the bathroom, install ground-fault circuit interrupters on all bathroom outlets. Some types of GFCI must be installed by an electrician, but portable, plug-in models are available at hardware stores for under thirty dollars. You just plug the unit into the outlet, and plug your appliance into that. The device will cut off the current if the appliance falls in water.

The CPSC also has reports of thousands of children (3,840 per year between 1985 and 1988) who were burned by curling irons. These and other hair appliances should be stored out of reach of children (even young toddlers can figure out how to plug them in), and placed out of reach to cool when you are finished with them.

Cleaning up

Parents are often so eager to protect their families from the nasty germs in the bathroom that they keep a number of even nastier cleaners within easy reach. Most of these contain disinfectants that can poison kids as well as germs. Toilet-bowl cleaners also contain acids that can burn skin and eyes. Many brands of cleanser contain silica, which is dangerous when inhaled. And should your child be unfortunate enough to mix cleanser containing chlorine bleach with another all-purpose cleaner, she could create a cloud of dangerous chlorine gas.

If you keep these products in the bathroom at all, they should be locked up. But I think it's preferable to store them in a locked room your child can't even get to, on a shelf too high for your child to reach. (Mine are in my dead-bolted washroom, on a shelf *I* can't even reach.)

An even better alternative, according to the Washington Toxics Coalition, an environmental organization that works to reduce society's reliance on toxic products, is to give up these cleaners altogether. If you have a mold or mildew problem in the bathroom, for instance, consider airing the room out more often to *prevent* the problem rather than using toxic cleaners to combat it.

Or try their "Safe Cleaning Kit," recipes for alternative cleaners that are safe anywhere you store them. With some baking soda, salt, distilled white vinegar, liquid soap, and vegetable oil, you can create cleaners that will handle almost any job. Try using baking soda and soap to scour the tub and tile. Add a little vinegar and you've got toilet-bowl cleaner. It takes a little more scrubbing, but the peace of mind is worth it. For a complete list of safe cleaning recipes, as well as a roster of safer commercial products, contact the Washington Toxics Coalition at (206) 632-1545.

Bad medicine

The medicine cabinet, despite its name, is not necessarily the best place to store your family's medications. Most people make an effort to keep their prescription medicines out of kids' way, but even aspirin can be poisonous in large doses. And your medicine cabinet might not be as out of reach as you think. They are generally located over the sink; in my house, we keep a stool in front of the sink to encourage our daughter's hand washing—a stool that also provides ready access to that cabinet.

Even products we don't consider medications may prove harmful. Some brands of mouthwash, for instance, contain as much as 14 to 27 percent alcohol, making a potentially lethal dose for a twenty-pound toddler as little as 4.5 ounces. Even *vitamins* can kill. (See "Medicines" for a complete guide to the dangers of prescription and over-the-counter drugs.)

Point bathroom hazards out to your child—even a child you think is too young to understand. Take your toddler in with you when you fill the tub. When you turn on the hot water, explain that it can burn her, and that she shouldn't touch it. Teach your child that she must never open medicine bottles—no matter where she finds them. Remind her not to run in the bathroom, and to be careful when standing in the tub. Teach her not to play with blow dryers and curling irons.

You can't lock your kids out of the bathroom to keep them away from its hazards. It's a room you *want* them to learn to use alone. Applying an ounce of prevention lets them use it safely.

Resources

"Tap Water Scalds Alert," "Prevent Child Drownings in the Home," "CPSC Warns of Drowning Hazard with Baby 'Supporting Ring' Devices," "Prevent Electrocutions: Use a Ground Fault Circuit Interrupter with Electric Heaters in the Bathroom," "New Hair Dryers Prevent Electrocutions," and "Young Children and Teens Burned by Hair Curling Irons," from the U.S. Consumer Product Safety Commission; (800) 638-2772.

"Scald Burn Facts," from the Gas Appliance Manufacturers Association. 1901 North Moore St., Arlington, VA 22209.

"Scald Burn Injury," from the National Safe Kids Campaign; (202) 884-4993.

"Protect Your Child," from the Alisa Ann Ruch Burn Foundation; (800) 242-BURN.

A Safer Home: Reducing Your Use of Hazardous Household Products, by Carl Woestwin, *Safer Cleaning Products,* by Jennie Goldberg, *Recipes for the Safe Cleaning Kit, and Buy Smart, Buy Safe: A Consumer Guide to Less-Toxic Products,* by Philip Dickey. Available through the Washington Toxics Coalition; (206) 632-1545.

BICYCLES

Heads up

Bicycle safety starts with teaching your child to use his head—covered with a helmet, of course. Two hundred and fifty kids a year are killed on their bikes, and another 400,000 are injured seriously enough for a trip to the hospital. Wearing a helmet reduces the risk of head injury—the leading cause of death in bicycle crashes—by as much as 85 percent, estimates the National Safe Kids Campaign. That makes helmets the single most important part of bike safety

Fit is priority one when buying a bicycle helmet. Don't choose one your child can "grow into." If the helmet doesn't fit properly, it won't protect her during an accident. It should be snug, but not tight, and should not rock front to back or side to side. Have your child try the helmet on to make sure it is comfortable and doesn't pinch. Once you've got a helmet that is basically the right size, you can use the sizing pads that come with most helmets to get the fit perfect. Add padding to the appropriate parts of the helmet until it exactly matches the shape of your child's head. Next, adjust the straps to make sure the helmet sits level, covering the top of the forehead. Your child should be able to fasten and unfasten the helmet easily, but the straps should stay snug even when you pull or twist the helmet itself.

It is also essential that your child's helmet meets safety standards. Look for a "Snell Approved" or "Meets ANSI Z90.4 Standard" sticker.

Finding your child the safest helmet on the market does no good if the kid won't wear it. So bring him to the store with you, and let him pick it out. It's best to get the helmet along with your child's first bike. That way he learns that bike and helmet go together. Let him choose whatever color he wants, and decorate it with stickers or decals to make it his own. Then insist that he wear his helmet every single time he rides his bike. Set a good example by *wearing your own helmet.*

Teach the whole family to keep their helmets clean with soap and water (never harsh chemicals that can damage them), and to avoid tossing or kicking their helmets, as this can damage them. Be sure to replace any helmet that has been in a crash (even if you don't see any damage) or any helmet your child outgrows.

The best bike

Your child's helmet should fit, and so should her bike. Never let your child ride a bicycle that is too large for her to handle. Riders should be able to touch both feet to the ground when they are seated on their bikes.

Do a simple weekly safety check with your child to make sure her bike is in proper riding order.

- Are the handlebars tight and straight, with grips on each handle?
- Do the brakes work smoothly and quickly? Are the hand brakes easy to squeeze?
- Spin the wheels and watch them turn. Do they wobble? (This means they are bent or loose.) Are all nuts tight? Are there loose or broken spokes?
- Are the tires firm and free from cuts, cracks, bulges, or foreign objects (like pieces of glass)?
- Is the chain clean and oiled, and properly tightened?
- Is the seat fastened securely? Does it wobble, twist, or slide?
- Are the reflectors clean? Are any broken or missing?
- Do the gears work properly and shift easily?
- Are the pedals tightly fastened? Do they spin smoothly?

Don't let your child ride her bike until any problems you find during the safety check are corrected. It is best to perform the check on the weekend, or some other day when you will have time to correct problems immediately. Don't do the check on a Monday night during a busy workweek and expect your kids to wait until the weekend for a chance to ride.

Rules to ride by

Unless you are seriously into biking yourself, your child will probably spend much of his riding time outside your direct supervision. The National Safe Kids Campaign says kids under age fourteen ride about 50 percent more than the average bicyclist (and account for more than one third of cyclists killed in traffic accidents), and unless you can keep up with them, you must teach them the importance of following traffic safety rules—even when Mom and Dad aren't looking.

Children under age ten should only ride on sidewalks or park bike paths, and should never ride at night. So for now, "Stay out of the street" is your mantra (right after, "Always wear your helmet."). Make sure your child knows exactly where she is and is not allowed to ride. Set clear boundaries so there is no doubt and no confusion.

Next, your young rider needs to learn the proper riding position. Children should ride sitting down on the seat, with both hands on the handlebars and both feet on the pedals at all times.

Teach your child always to ride single file, and to stay alert, looking and listening for hazards and slowing down at driveways to watch for cars. If you allow your child to cross any street, she should know to stop at intersections, get off her bike, and walk it across.

Kids older than ten who have mastered safe riding on the sidewalk can progress to riding in the street (always as far to the right as possible). However, your child still needs a clear set of boundaries so he knows where it is safe to ride and where it is not. Buy or draw a map of your neighborhood, and mark your child's safe riding area clearly. Then take the time to go for a ride or walk together to reinforce the outer limits. Even within the boundaries, make sure he knows enough to avoid such unsafe areas as vacant lots, parking lots, construction sites, and railroad tracks. And even at this age, children should not ride at night.

Teach your child the hand signals for right turn (left arm turned upward), left turn (left arm out straight), and stop (left arm turned downward), and how to read traffic signs and signals. He will also need to learn to watch out for cars and pedestrians sharing the roadway. If your child is riding to school, make sure he has a basket or backpack to hold his books so he can keep both hands on the handlebars. And teach your child never to ride more than one person to a bicycle.

Set an example

The best way to teach your children good bicycle safety habits is to get out there and ride with them. When your children see you wearing your helmet and obeying the rules of the road, they'll naturally follow suit (at least while you're around).

Once they're on their way, it's time for you to follow them, watching to see that they stay alert and ride correctly. It's great exercise—and you might even have fun!

Resources _____

San Diego County's Heads Up Bicycle Safety Program: Kindergarten-Second Grade Coloring & Activity Book, Third-Eighth Grades, and Instructor's & PTA Guide to Bicycle Safety: Kindergarden-Eighth Grades, from the San Diego Safe Kids Coalition.

"Traffic Safety Outlook: Bicycle Safety," from the National Highway Traffic Safety Administration; (800) 424-9393.

"Kids Speak Out on Bike Helmets," "Back to School Safety Alert," and "Night Bike Riders at Risk," from the U.S. Consumer Product Safety Commission; (800) 638-2772.

"Bicycle Helmets," Associated Press news bulletin, February 13, 1996.

Safe Kids Are No Accident: A Traffic Safety Magazine for Kids, "Bicycle Injury Fact Sheet," and "Lou and His Friends Have Something Important to Tell You," from the National Safe Kids Campaign; (202) 884-4993.

BIRTHDAY PARTIES

If you're a kid, it doesn't get much better than a birthday party—especially if the party is yours. Most parents do a lot of planning and work to get ready for the big day, and some safety planning should be part of the job.

The party place

If you're having the party at home and you've been careful about babyproofing, you won't have to worry much about your little guests getting into anything they shouldn't, according to Susan Tully, M.D., with the American Academy of Pediatrics Commission on injury prevention. "If your home is safe for your child, it should be safe for other children," Tully explains. However, if some of the children at the party are younger than yours, you may have to do a bit of backtracking (see the appropriate babyproofing checklist). This means it's a good idea to know exactly who's coming to the party.

If you're having the party someplace else—a park, skating rink, or other party venue—you'll need to check the place out ahead of time. "Make sure the place doesn't have anything you wouldn't have in your home," says Tully. If it's a park, make sure the playground is safe. (See "Playgrounds.") If it's some other sort of venue, look things over, ask what has been done to ensure the children's safety, and find out if they provide additional supervision. Make sure any activities offered will be appropriate for the ages of the children at the party.

Decorations

Balloons are the cornerstone of most birthday decorating schemes, but they are also the most common cause of choking deaths in kids. (See "Toys.") They aren't recommended as party favors for children under five. And if they're part of the decor, hang 'em high, where they aren't likely to get broken and become dangerous. The editors of *Home Safe & Sound,* a yearly publication devoted to home safety, recommend Mylar balloons as a safer alternative.

In the bag

Another area where you have to be careful of choking hazards is in the planning of goody bags. The Consumer Product Safety Commission requires warning labels on toys that pose a choking hazard for children under age three, but many of the "party favor" type toys on the market are manufactured in other countries, and hazardous items occasionally make it to store shelves unmarked. Avoid putting any toy that would fit through a toilet-paper tube into a goody bag for a child under age three. Also stay away from any toys with sharp edges or brittle parts that could break into sharp pieces.

Toys with long strings are also not a good idea for kids under three. They could become tangled around a child's neck and choke her. Even the goody bag itself is a potential hazard—so make sure it's a paper one. About fifteen children a year choke to death on plastic bags, says the CPSC.

Supervision

Having enough adults on hand to keep track of a group of excited children is the main problem at birthday parties, according to Tully. "I had a rule in my house that worked very well. You could have the same number of people at your birthday party as the number of years old you were." This, she explains, kept the number of guests from getting too high until the children were older.

If you can't help inviting the whole class, the editors of *Home Safe & Sound* suggest recruiting some of the parents to stay and help. For a group of three-to-five-year-olds, they recommend at least one adult for every five children. You'll need fewer grown-ups as the kids get older.

Games

Planning plenty of games and activities will give guests less free time and make them easier to supervise. When the kids do have free time (while the first guests are arriving, or the last are leaving), setting up a designated spot and a designated activity (e.g., making their own party hats, etc.) will keep them busy, says *Home Safe & Sound*.

There are also plenty of fun party games for all ages. If you're going to play active games that involve running, jumping, or dancing, be sure to let parents know ahead of time so they can dress their children in tennis shoes. Party shoes aren't safe to play in because they don't give enough traction.

Piñatas are a fun birthday tradition that has been adopted by many families. If your child is old enough for a piñata (which means she is old enough to swing a big stick around with her eyes closed), set up a designated area far away from the action, marked off by chalk, string, or some other means so that children know where it is safe to stand. Fill the piñata with wrapped candy, but be careful if there are younger children around. They may get their hands on a piece of the candy and choke.

Glorious food

Another time you'll have to keep a good watch on the children is when the cake comes out with candles a-burning. Make it a rule that the cake doesn't come out until everyone is sitting down, suggests *Safe & Sound*. Kids love to lick the frosting off the extinguished candles, but make them count to thirty first so that no one gets burned.

Be careful when choosing and preparing children's food for a party. If possible, serve foods that are precut into chokeproof pieces. Avoid foods like nuts or whole grapes, and slice hot dogs and bananas vertically up the middle before serving. (See also

"Food.") It's also a good idea to make the kids sit down to eat. Kids who are talking and jumping around while they eat are more likely to choke.

The editors of *Home Safe & Sound* also recommend checking with parents ahead of time to make sure there are no food allergies among your guests.

The presents

The grand finale of any good party is the opening of the presents. And while your excited birthday kid digs in, your job (besides clearing away the torn paper, keeping the thank-you-note list, and taking pictures) is to make sure any plastic wrap pulled off of any plaything is picked up and put in the trash before it finds its way into anyone's mouth.

If there are younger children at the party, you may have to keep watch to make sure they don't get their hands on toys meant for older children—which could be a danger to the little ones. Having special little-kid goody bags will help discourage them while preventing hurt feelings.

If you plan things right, the only stress you'll have to deal with is the stress caused by your baby getting a whole year older. You won't have to worry about anyone getting hurt.

Resources

"Safety at Birthday Parties," from the editors of *Home Safe & Sound*, a free annual guide to home safety. For a copy, send $1.50 for shipping and handling to Home Safe & Sound, Free Offer, P.O. Box 6960, Villa Park, IL 60181, or call (630) 832-3830.

The U.S. Consumer Product Safety Commission; (800) 638-2772.

CAR SAFETY

There was a green light at the intersection a block from my apartment, but suddenly a truck was in front of me. I heard a crash, and felt a jolt, and my car was spinning all over the road. I curled up, trying to shield my pregnant stomach.

The car, which finally skidded to a stop, was totaled. The baby was fine. And that terrifying afternoon was my family's guarantee that none of us would ever ride without a seat belt.

Over the past decade, technological improvements like shoulder belts, air bags, and especially child safety seats have saved more than 65,200 lives. But amazingly, only 67 percent of car passengers wear their safety belts, according to the National Highway Traffic Safety Administration, and only about 65 percent of parents strap their kids into car safety seats—even though it's the law.

A shocking 1,374 children are killed and 269,000 injured in cars *every year*. Car crashes kill more kids than any other hazard, causing 45 percent of all accidental children's deaths, says the National Safe Kids Campaign.

Passenger safety

You need to start thinking about car safety before your baby is born, because that unborn baby is riding along in utero. Many pregnant women don't want to wear seat belts because the belts feel uncomfortable (as do most things you wear during pregnancy), or because they are afraid the belt will harm their baby. But my safety belt saved my baby's life.

The American College of Obstetrics and Gynecology and Safety-BeltSafe say pregnant women should buckle up, with their lap belt low, under the baby, and the shoulder belt across the center of the chest.

Take a seat

You'll also need to think about a car seat, because you'll need one for the trip home from the hospital. Though many hospitals have a loan program, I recommend buying a seat well before the due date so you have plenty of time to master the installation process (no easy feat).

Either an infant safety seat (a small, easy-to-carry version you can use until your baby weighs about twenty pounds) or a convertible seat (which faces rearward for an infant and forward for a child up to about thirty pounds) is safe for your newborn. The infant seat, however, may be a better fit. In either type of seat, your baby should sit in the backseat of the car, facing backward. If you plan to use a convertible seat for a new baby, choose one with a five-point harness (straps that attach over the shoulders, at the sides, and between the legs), rather than a shield. The shield often provides a poor fit for a newborn.

Never, under any circumstances, ride an infant in a rear-facing car seat in the front seat of a car with a passenger-side air bag. During a crash, the air bag will explode out of the dashboard at 200 mph, and strike the car seat with enough force to kill your baby. As of January 1996, at least thirty children had been killed by air bags, according to the National Highway Traffic Safety Administration. One of these was a twenty-day-old infant killed in a car traveling just twenty-three miles per hour.

Once your child weighs twenty pounds, you can turn the seat around to face forward, but the backseat is still the safest spot in the car.

Children who weigh forty pounds and have outgrown their car seat can use a booster seat, which provides added protection by helping the car's lap and shoulder belts fit correctly.

If you are buying a new seat, fill out and return the registration card so you will be notified by the manufacturer if the seat is recalled for safety reasons. Never use a pre-owned or borrowed seat that is more than ten years old or has been in a crash. Make sure all manufacturer's labels are intact and legible.

Whether your seat is new or used, if you have not filled out and returned the manufacturer's registration card, check to see that the seat has not been recalled. To find out, call the National Highway Traffic Safety Administration hotline, (800) 424-9393, or the Consumer Product Safety Commission hotline, (800) 638-2772. You will need to know the manufacturer's name, the model name or number of the seat, and the manufacture date. Don't use any car seat without having this important information.

Sitting pretty

Every year, SafetyBeltSafe U.S.A. provides free car-seat inspections to help parents make sure they are using their seats properly. In 1995, they found that as many as nine out of ten were not. An incorrectly installed seat won't protect your child in a crash, so use these safety tips to avoid common mistakes:

- *Read the labels* on your car seat, your car's seat belts and your car visor, and follow any special installation instructions you find there. These labels may tell you to use a special locking clip or buckle when installing a car seat. Call your auto dealer and/or the manufacturer of your seat (you'll usually find the toll-free number on the instruction label) if you are confused by the installation instructions.
- *Make sure your seat belt stays tightly fastened around your car seat.* To get a really tight fit, push the car seat down into the seat padding with your knee while you fasten the belt. Then give the seat a yank. Pull hard from side to side and see if the belt loosens.

    If you are using a lap belt to secure the seat and it loosens, it may be because the latch plate is tilting (because that's how they are adjusted). Try snugging up the belt, turning the latch plate over, and buckling it upside down. This will keep the belt from tilting and loosening up.

If you are using a lap/shoulder belt and it comes loose, you may need to use a locking clip. Some lap/shoulder belts stay loose except in a crash or sudden stop, and these are not good for holding a car seat snugly. Locking clips, which come with most safety seats, can be attached to the belt near the latch plate to make it hold tight. The installation instructions on your car seat should cover proper use of a locking clip.

If you need to use a car seat in a front seat where the lap/shoulder belts are attached to the door, or if the lap and shoulder belts are sewn to the latch plate, you will need to follow special procedures. For door-attached belts, call your auto dealership and ask them to install a lap belt that will hold your car seat. If lap and shoulder belts are sewn to the latch plate, you'll need to get a special heavy-duty locking clip from your dealer to shorten the belt to a length that holds your car seat securely. A regular locking clip is not strong enough to do this safely, so don't try to use one.

• *If you have questions about using locking clips or installing your car seat, call the Auto Safety Hotline; (800) 424-9393.*
• *Now make sure your child is properly belted into the seat.*

Infant/toddler seats: Dress your child in clothes that allow the car seat's harness to be fastened properly between the legs and to keep the straps snugly over the shoulders. The car seat's straps should never go above an infant's shoulders. An infant seat should face the rear of the car, and should be tilted at a forty-five-degree angle. Place a rolled-up towel under the front edge of the seat if it is tipped so high your baby's head flops forward, but don't tilt the seat too much. Doing this could allow your baby to be thrown over the top of the seat in a crash.

If you plan to bundle your child up in a blanket, put the blanket on *after* buckling her in. Putting the blanket under the harness can interfere with the straps. If your baby slumps over in the seat, tuck rolled towels or blankets beside her to hold her comfortably.

Harness straps should lie flat, never twisted, and the retainer clip (the metal piece that holds the two straps perpendicular to each other) should be placed so that the straps fit properly. A colleague of mine has a two-year-old who often slides the retainer clip on her car seat down, leaving the straps dangerously off her shoulders. Adding a second retainer clip, installed upside down, makes this maneuver too difficult to be fun.

Booster seats: If you are riding an older child in a booster seat and using only a lap belt, the booster must have a shield. Boosters without shields are okay for use with lap and shoulder belts. If your child's ears reach above the top of the seat back, use a booster with a higher back.

Give 'em the belt

The rules for safe seat-belt use are much simpler than the complicated installation of car seats. So once your child is big enough for the belt to fit properly, you've got it easy. All you have to remember is:

- Buckle your child in every single time they ride anywhere in the car. The majority of crashes happen within twenty-five miles of home at speeds below 35 mph, and your child has an 85 percent better chance of surviving an accident if she is wearing a seat belt.
- Your child's lap belt should fit low, over the hips, so the strong bones of the legs and pelvis can absorb the shock of a crash. Letting the lap belt ride up over the stomach could damage internal organs if crash impact causes her to be thrown forward.
- The shoulder belt should go across the center of the chest and over the shoulder—never across the neck or under the arm. This could also cause internal damage during a crash.

There are a number of products now on the market to help adjust the fit of shoulder straps for children. The manufacturers say they have crash-tested their products and found that they provide superior protection to seat belts alone. However, the National Highway Traffic Safety Administration, while it doesn't call these products unsafe, cannot recommend them.

"We don't know if they're a good idea," says spokesperson Tim Hurd. "Safety-belt systems differ from car to car, so we have to refer people to the car manufacturers." Hurd goes on to explain that these products alter the manufacturers' intended angles of the safety belt, and should not be used unless your manufacturer has tested and recommends them for use in your car. If your manufacturer does not recommend them, Hurd advises parents to use a booster seat instead.

- Never buckle more than one child into a safety belt. Two people belted in together could actually injure each other during a crash.

Air bags

Air bags are popping up all over. (Almost all cars and trucks will come equipped with both driver's and passenger-side air bags by 1998, according to the American Coalition for Traffic Safety.) They have saved many lives, but they have also taken a few. The fact is that these devices, rather than billowing forth like fluffy pillows (the way they look on TV) actually explode out of the steering wheel or dashboard at about 200 mph. The force of air bags deploying has killed at least thirty children, and the rate continues to rise as more passenger-side air bags are installed in new cars.

These children generally die of massive brain injuries they receive when the air bag explodes and hits them in the head. Other victims include infants in rear-facing car seats. When the bag hits the seat, its lethal force is carried by the seat directly to the baby's head.

Manufacturers are working on cutoff switches for cars with no backseats so parents can disable air bags when they are carrying an infant or child in the passenger seat. Still others are developing air bags that deploy with less force, and "smart" air bags that can sense when an infant carrier or child is in the passenger seat, and not deploy. These products could be in use in the next four to five years, according to the National Highway Traffic Safety Administration.

But until they are, the bottom line is that kids and air bags don't mix. The safest place for any child under age twelve is in the backseat, in a properly fitting seat belt or approved child safety seat. *Infants in rear-facing car seats should never ride in the front seat of cars with a passenger-side air bag.* And if possible, neither should any child.

The bottom line

Above all, remember that the safest place in the car for your child is never in your arms. If your car crashes even at twenty miles per hour, your twenty-five-pound baby would fly out of your arms with five hundred pounds of force. Even if you could hold on, your body would then be thrown forward on top of the baby with more than one ton of force.

Teach your child from the very start that they belong in a car seat or seat belt when they are traveling in *anyone's* car. Even young toddlers can learn this. When my daughter was about two and a half, we were driving to a party with a friend and her baby. I had put Lauren in her car seat, and then hurried around to help my friend buckle in her baby's seat. When I got in and started the engine, Lauren started to howl.

"Mommy," she cried, "you forgot to buckle my seat!"

Resources

"What You Need to Know About Airbags," from the American Coalition for Traffic Safety, Inc.; (703) 243-7501.

"Passenger-side Air Bags Could Injure Infants Riding Facing the Rear of the Car," "Children and Air Bags," "Are You Using It Right?", "Traffic Safety Outlook: Child Passenger Safety," "How to Keep Your Child in One Piece," *AutoFacts,* Winter 1994, and *Child Passenger Safety Tips,* from the U.S. Department of Transportation National Highway Traffic Safety Administration; (800) 424-9393.

All Kids Ride Safe Fact Kit, from the Allstate Foundation and the American Academy of Pediatrics.

"Airbag Dangers," Associated Press news bulletin, September 12, 1995.

"Child Safety Seats: How Safe?", *Consumer Reports,* September 1995, pp. 580-584.

"Air-Bag-Associated Fatal Injuries to Infants and Children Riding in Front Passenger Seats—United States," Morbidity and Mortality Weekly Report from the U.S. Centers for Disease Control and Prevention, November 17, 1995.

"Safety Belt Roulette," "The Perfect Gift," and "Protect Your Baby Now and Later," from SafetyBeltSafe U.S.A.; (310) 673-2666.

"Motor Vehicle Occupant Injury," fact sheet from the National Safe Kids Campaign; (202) 884-4993.

CARBON MONOXIDE

This colorless, odorless gas kills three hundred people in the United States every year. When fuel-burning appliances (stoves, water heaters, furnaces) and fireplaces are operating correctly, only low levels of CO are produced. But if one of these appliances malfunctions, levels can rise and become dangerous. At high levels, carbon monoxide poisons the body by limiting the blood's capacity to carry oxygen, and can kill in hours or minutes.

Since children have higher metabolisms, they require more oxygen, and thus face increased danger from CO poisoning, according to Dr. Mark Bayer, medical director of the Connecticut Poison Control Center. Carbon-monoxide poisoning can lead to neurological, learning, and developmental problems in children, and miscarriage and stillbirth for pregnant women. And CO levels in the fetus continue to rise even after the mother is well, according to the November 1, 1993, issue of *American Family Physician*.

This means households with pregnant women and children should pay special attention to the Consumer Product Safety Commission recommendation that every home be equipped with at least one CO detector, located near the bedroom.

You need a carbon-monoxide detector if:

- You have gas or fuel-burning appliances (the stove, hot water heater, dryer, furnace) in your home.
- You have a fireplace.

Detecting a good detector

The July 1995 issue of *Consumer Reports* contains a thorough look at carbon-monoxide detectors. Their testers recommend buying a detector with:

- An alarm that stops automatically when fresh air clears the CO.
- A hush or reset button to silence the alarm immediately when it sounds (so you can shut the horn off if you suspect a false alarm; the unit should sound again if carbon monoxide levels are truly high).
- A digital display or warning light.
- A light that tells you the power is on.

- A horn that sounds an eighty-five-decibel alarm when CO levels are dangerously high.
- A test button to verify the unit's electronic elements are working.
- A power cord at least six feet long on plug-in models.
- A battery sensor pack on battery-operated models.
- Underwriters Laboratory listing.

Consumer Reports also mentions that, of the dozen types of detectors they tested, they found the plug-in units "superior," performing most consistently. They found the battery-powered units less responsive to high CO levels. Also, because their sensors accumulate carbon monoxide over time, battery-powered units may sound nuisance alarms during prolonged spells of urban air pollution. According to the magazine, you should be able to purchase a good quality detector for under fifty dollars.

Underwriters Laboratories Inc., which rates detectors, advises against placing your unit directly on top of or directly across from fuel-burning appliances, which will emit some CO when initially turned on, causing false alarms.

A kit from Heads Up! products also allows you to test your detector with real carbon monoxide. The kit contains an ampoule of concentrated CO gas so you can safely see if your unit will respond to elevated carbon-monoxide levels. The manufacturer recommends testing your detector upon installation, and annually thereafter. Their tester retails for around six dollars, and is available by calling Heads Up! at (800) 548-2117.

An ounce of prevention

To keep levels of carbon monoxide from building up in your home, you should have your heating system and all fuel-burning appliances inspected annually to make sure they are working properly (your local gas company will usually do this free of charge). If you have a fireplace, have the chimney cleaned and inspected as well.

You should also keep an eye out for signs that an appliance or your chimney isn't working right. These include rusting or water streaking on your chimney, loose or missing furnace panels, sooting around your fuel-burning appliances, loose or disconnected vent or chimney connections, debris or soot falling from your chimney, loose masonry on your chimney, moisture on the insides of your windows, decreasing hot-water supply (indicating your gas water heater is malfunctioning), or a furnace that doesn't heat the house the way it once did.

And you should avoid certain practices that can fill your house with carbon monoxide. Never burn charcoal indoors or in a garage. Never use your gas range or oven to heat your home, and never use a fuel-burning space heater in a closed room. And never leave a car running in a garage.

Warning signs of CO poisoning

Initial symptoms of carbon monoxide poisoning are easily mistaken for the flu:

- Dizziness
- Fatigue
- Headache
- Nausea
- Irregular breathing

Moderate poisoning mimics food poisoning, with symptoms such as nausea, vomiting, abdominal cramps, and diarrhea, and also causes shortness of breath and confusion. Severe poisoning can lead to coma, shock, loss of vision, symptoms resembling a stroke or heart attack, and eventually death.

If a member of your family begins to experience any of these symptoms and you suspect it could be from carbon monoxide, take them outside in the fresh air. If they feel better outside, but symptoms return when they return to the house, it might be CO poisoning. Get everyone out of the house, turn off all fuel-burning appliances, open all windows and doors, and air out the house. Don't run any fuel-burning appliance until you can have all appliances and your fireplace checked and locate the source of the problem.

Take anyone who has been sick to the doctor and explain that you suspect CO poisoning. Treatment may be required even if the person is already feeling better.

Resources

"The Senseless Killer," from the Alisa Ann Ruch Burn Foundation; (800) 242-BURN.

"Prevent Carbon Monoxide Poisoning," from the Los Angeles Regional Drug and Poison Information Center; (800) 777-6476.

JL Sims Company, Inc., Heads Up! products; http://headsupusa.com or (800) 496-2144.

"Be Alert to Signs of Carbon Monoxide Poisoning," from Underwriters Laboratories Inc.; (708) 272-8800.

"Carbon Monoxide Detectors Can Save Lives," from the U.S. Consumer Product Safety Commission; (800) 638-2772.

"CO Detectors: An Early Warning," *Consumer Reports*, July 1995, pp 466-467.

CHILD CARE

One of the hardest things you will ever do as a parent is leave your child in the care of someone else. You'll worry whether she is happy. You'll worry that he is missing you. But if you've done your homework and made quality child-care arrangements, you won't have worries about whether your children are safe.

These guidelines are for people considering either home-based day care, or a child-care center or preschool. If you're planning to have someone care for your children in your home, the "Babysitter" chapter has some guidelines that apply.

You should also keep in mind that these guidelines only cover safety issues, and it takes much more than safety guidelines to help you find a place where your child can learn, grow, and feel truly cared for. Any of the organizations listed in the resources section of this chapter can help you fill in the rest of the requirements.

The facility

You can't judge a book by its cover, but you can tell a lot about a day-care center before you even get out of the car. Take a look at the building itself. Is it clean and well maintained? Is the landscaping pleasant and kept up? How's the neighborhood? Since your child will be spending quite a bit of time here, you should be concerned with such things as nearby traffic, the noise level, sources of pollution, and other environmental hazards such as asbestos or high radon levels.

The center should have an open-door policy that allows parents to visit at any time, announced or not. But access to the building and yard or playground should be controlled. No one should be able to stroll onto the grounds and into areas where children are cared for without first encountering a caregiver or other staff member. Anyone who is not a parent authorized to pick up or drop off their child should immediately be questioned about their identity and their business at the center.

Caregivers should never allow *anyone* to take a child from the facility without prior written authorization from the custodial parent. The school should also ask you to give them the names and telephone numbers of two or three people allowed to pick up your child in an emergency.

If the center or caregiver is licensed or accredited, they should be happy to show you documentation to this effect. Check the dates on these documents, and ask about those that might have expired. Centers that are licensed or accredited have generally taken measures to meet a specific set of standards, but the presence of a license or certificate of accreditation does not guarantee that those standards have been maintained. So always give the place the once-over yourself.

Classroom safety

Any classroom or area where your child will be spending time should have an open floor plan so that the children are easily visible at all times. Watch out for hidden nooks or corners—especially areas where children could be kept alone with an adult. This includes bathrooms.

The majority of the stuff in the classroom or child-care area should be age-appropriate to the children being cared for. Furniture should be child size and sturdy. Playthings should suit the age of the players. (See "Toys.") Pets should be kid-friendly (see "Pets") and their cages should be clean.

Check for basic childproofing measures, including ones you might have taken at home. Look for such things as furniture with sharp edges, dangerous objects, medicines or toxic substances left within children's reach, ungated stairways, and exposed electrical outlets.

All carpets and flooring should be in good repair to prevent falls, and openable windows should be childproofed and screened. (See "Windows.")

The area where your child is cared for should not be used for any other business or purpose so babyproofing measures can be maintained.

Outdoor safety

The first thing to check out in the play yard is the fence. There should be one that covers the entire perimeter of the yard. It should be in good condition, and any gates should have sturdy locks.

Porches, steps, and walkways should be clean, clear, and in good repair. They should be kept free of ice or water, excessive weeds or brush (to prevent allergies), and loose objects that might cause falls.

Playground equipment should be age-appropriate and in good condition, with adequate ground cover and soft-fall zones. (See "Playgrounds.")

Pools should be separate from buildings and the main play yard, and completely surrounded by a nonclimbable fence with a locking gate. Children should never be allowed unsupervised in the pool area, or any other area where there is any body of water (buckets, hot tubs, wading pools, and pails included). Children can drown in under three minutes in less than three inches of water. Dangerous roughhousing should not be permitted near the pool, and nonwater toys should not be allowed in the pool area. (See "Swimming/Pools.")

Staff qualifications

Anyone who will care for your children should be screened for criminal history in sexual or physical assault against children, emotional instability, and substance abuse. They should have experience caring for small children and some knowledge of child development.

Caregivers should also be certified in pediatric first aid that includes rescue breathing and first aid for choking. They should be secure enough in their knowledge of first aid that they won't hesitate to take the proper action in an emergency situation, and should also know how to deal with nonemergency stuff like bandaging scraped knees and icing down bumps on the head. If there is a pool on the premises, caregivers should also be trained in basic water safety and CPR.

Supervision

The facility you are considering should have enough caregivers on staff so that children can be supervised at all times—even when sleeping. The child-caregiver ratio should also be low enough to keep staff members from getting stressed out and losing control. Caregivers trying to cope with excessive demands have trouble providing enough supervision to ensure safety. Low ratios are especially important for infants and toddlers, who need an adult's help to escape the building during a fire or other emergency.

Home-based caregivers without an assistant should take in no more than six children, with no more than two of these under age two, including the caregiver's own children under age six.

This table gives the ratio for children in day-care centers:

Birth to 24 months:	3:1, maximum 6 children
25 to 30 months:	4:1, maximum 8 children
31 to 35 months:	5:1, maximum 10 children
3-year-olds:	7:1, maximum 14 children
4-to-5 year-olds:	8:1, maximum 16 children
6-to-8 year-olds:	10:1, maximum 20 children
9-to-12 year-olds:	12:1, maximum 24 children

Sanitation

Hand washing helps prevent the spread of germs and illnesses major and minor. Staff members should always wash their hands before preparing, handling, or serving food, after using the bathroom, helping a child use the bathroom, or changing diapers. Children should be taught to wash their hands after using the bathroom, before and after eating, and after handling pets. Caregivers should reinforce lessons about the proper use of running water, soap, and disposable paper towels for cleaning hands, and supervise children to be sure they are doing it right.

Toys should also be kept clean and free of germs. Infant/toddler toys should be cleaned and disinfected daily, and toys in rooms with older children should be cleaned at least weekly. The only non-washable toys allowed in infant/toddler rooms should be personal items that are not shared between children.

All bedding should be changed whenever it is soiled or wet. Infant bedding should be changed daily, and bedding for older children should be changed at least weekly.

Floors should be swept or vacuumed daily, and noncarpeted floors should be mopped with a disinfectant solution.

The bathroom should be cleaned and sanitized at least daily, and equipment used here should not be used in any other part of the facility. There should be a separate diaper-changing area that can be cleaned and sanitized after each change, and dirty diapers should be stored away from children.

Illness

The staff should always be on the lookout for changes in behavior or signs of illness such as fever, rash, or complaints of pain. If a child is too sick to participate in activities, or has an infectious condition that might be spread to other children, she should be sent home.

Likewise, teachers should not be at the center if they have a bug that could spread to the children, or if their illness might hinder them from keeping the children safe. A teacher with a severe sinus headache, for instance, is not contagious, but might not be able to focus his attention well enough to properly supervise playground activities.

Immunization requirements should be enforced for both children and staff.

Emergency preparedness

Each room should have two emergency exits that are kept clear of obstructions at all times. Doors should not be locked or fastened in any way that prevents escape from the building during an emergency. Door hardware in areas used by school-age children should be within reach of the child. In centers, only panic hardware (which can be opened by applying pressure in the direction of travel) should be used on exterior doors.

There should be smoke detectors and fire extinguishers with posted operating instructions on every floor. Detectors should be located six or twelve inches below ceiling level, tested monthly, and the batteries replaced annually. If the home or center has natural gas heating or appliances, it should also have carbon-monoxide detectors.

The center should have two first-aid kits, one to be taken on field trips. Each kit should be accessible to all caregivers but inaccessible to children. Inventory should be conducted monthly. (See "First-Aid Kits.") Posted emergency instructions should cover first aid, CPR, and choking.

The center should have a plan for emergency transportation to a hospital, and a caregiver should be able to accompany the child to the hospital and stay with her until the parent arrives. There should be enough available staff to guarantee the adequate supervision of children who remain at the school. Emergency information should be kept for each child, including a release form and list of allergies.

A school should have a written plan for evacuation in the event of a disaster, and at least a seventy-two-hour supply of food and water stored for each child. Provisions should include formula for babies, disposable diapers, wipes, and prescription medications, extra clothes, blankets, family photos, etc.

Evacuation drills should be practiced on a monthly basis for tornadoes during tornado season, every six months for earthquakes, and yearly for hurricanes. Fire evacuation drills should be practiced monthly all year, at different times of the day, including naptime.

Resources

Caring for Our Children, National Health and Safety Performance Standards: Guidelines for Out-of-Home Child Care Programs, by the American Public Health Association and the American Academy of Pediatrics; (847) 981-5100.

"The Right Path to Quality Child Care," from the National Child Care Association; (800) 543-7161.

"Family Day Care: A Guide for Parents Using or Seeking Home-Based Childcare," from the Children's Foundation; (202) 347-3300.

"Parental Guidelines in Case You Are Considering Daycare," from the National Center for Missing and Exploited Children; (703) 235-3900.

"How to Choose a Good Early Childhood Program," from the National Association for the Education of Young Children; (800) 424-2460.

Finding Quality Child care: What Every Parent Needs to Know," a video produced by Quartet Creative Services; (800) 859-5105.

"Parents' Quality Checklist," from Child Care Aware; (800) 424-2246.

CHILD'S BEDROOM

Your child may not spend much time in his room, but if you do your best to make it a safe haven, you can relax a bit more during those rare moments of sleep and play.

Sleep, baby, sleep

Newborns spend about eighteen hours a day sleeping, making a safe bassinet or cradle an essential—especially since you're likely to pass out from new-parent exhaustion as soon as those little eyes close. About 740 babies a year are treated in emergency rooms because they are hurt when their bassinet or cradle tips over, according to the Consumer Product Safety Commission. Other babies are injured when the bottom of the bassinet or cradle breaks, so follow the manufacturer's guidelines and don't use the bed for babies who are too big or heavy.

- Choose an infant bed with a sturdy bottom and a wide, stable base to prevent tip-overs.
- If the legs fold, make sure they can be locked securely so they do not fold up while your baby is in the bed.

     Note: You can avoid these first two hazards completely by using an old-fashioned cradle that sits close to the ground. Ours was a heavy wooden model no more than three inches off the floor, with long flat rockers across the bottom so the cradle wouldn't tip over. It fit nicely at the foot of our bed, and I could rock the baby back to sleep at night by pushing the rocker with my foot.
- All surfaces of the bed should be smooth, with no protruding staples, bolts, or sharp edges.
- The mattress should be firm and fit snugly into the cradle or bassinet. You should not be able to fit more than two fingers between the edge of the mattress and the bed frame. Any more space might allow your baby to be trapped between the mattress and frame, and suffocate.
- All screws and bolts holding the bed together should be tight.

Crib notes

Fifty babies a year die in the bed their parents have tucked them into, says the CPSC. Thousands more are injured severely enough to be taken to the hospital. New cribs are designed to prevent these tragedies, but many parents either buy used cribs or borrow older cribs from friends. Whether your crib is new or used, it should meet the following safety specifications:

- Slats should be spaced no more than 2 3/8 inches apart so a baby's head cannot fit through and get caught. *If you absolutely have to use a crib that does not meet this requirement, the CPSC recommends attaching bumper pads securely all the way around the crib.* Never use a crib with missing slats.

- Corner posts should not be more than one-sixteenth of an inch higher than the end panels so baby's clothing cannot get caught on them and strangle her. *If your crib has taller corner posts, you should saw them off at the level of the end panels, and sand the area smooth.*
- Many older cribs have decorative cutouts that could trap a baby's head. Avoid these. Your crib's end panels should be solid.
- The mattress should fit snugly so the baby can't become trapped between the mattress and the frame. You shouldn't be able to fit more than two fingers between the mattress side and the frame. *If your mattress is too small and you can't replace it with one that fits snugly, stuff rolled towels in the space between the mattress and the frame. Fill the entire open space.*
- The mattress support should attach securely to the frame.
- The entire crib should be free of loose, missing, broken, or improperly installed screws, brackets, or other parts.
- The crib's paint should be in good condition—not cracked or peeling—and there should be no splinters or rough edges anywhere on the crib.

Once you have found a safe crib, make sure you use it safely:

- Always keep the drop side up when your baby is in the crib. Make sure the drop-side latches hold securely and cannot easily be released by the baby.
- If you use bumper pads, make sure they fit around the entire crib and tie or snap into place with at least six straps—one at each corner post and one in the middle of each side. If the pads tie into place, trim off excess cord to keep the baby from becoming tangled in it. Once your baby can pull up to a standing position,

remove the bumpers so she won't use them to climb out of the crib.

- Never place your crib near window blinds, draperies, or wall decorations with long cords, because your baby could get them wrapped around his neck and strangle. Never hang anything with a long cord on or near the crib.
- Toys that hang by a string over the crib should be out of reach of the baby. Make sure any crib toys that stretch across the crib are attached securely at both ends, and take them out as soon as your baby can push herself up on her arms and legs or is five months old.
- Move your baby into a bed when she is thirty-five inches tall or two years old—or as soon as she shows signs of being able to climb out of the crib.

Blankies and stuff

Whether your baby is sleeping in a bassinet or has graduated to a cradle, safe bedding is as important as a safe place to sleep. A firm mattress is the foundation of a safe bed.

The mattress, pad, and a fitted sheet are all that belong under your baby. Never put babies to sleep on top of a pillow, quilt, or blanket. A two-year study completed by the CPSC in 1995 found that nearly a third of the six thousand infants who die of Sudden Infant Death Syndrome each year are found lying facedown on soft bedding. The theory is that the bedding traps carbon dioxide, causing the baby to suffocate when he rebreathes it. Though this has not been identified as a *cause* of SIDS, the SIDS Alliance recommends putting babies to sleep on their backs or sides on firm bedding.

Never use dry-cleaning bags or other thin plastics as mattress covers. The plastic may cling to your child's face and suffocate him. Instead use a rubber sheet or rubberized mattress pad.

Also avoid using infant cushions, which have been banned by

the CPSC, or other beanbag-style items as a bed for your baby. They can mold themselves to your baby's face and suffocate him.

Changes

Your most frequent visits to your baby's room will probably be to change diapers and—if you haven't changed the diapers in time— to change clothes. The Juvenile Products Manufacturers Association recommends using a sturdy table certified by them, with safety straps to keep your baby from falling.

I recommend abandoning changing tables altogether and changing and dressing your child someplace closer to the ground. (See "Diapering.")

"Pails" by comparison

Once you've got the dirty stuff off, you've got to have a place to put it. Diaper pails are a sad and smelly fact of baby life, but they can also be a hazard if you do not keep them tightly latched. If your baby falls headfirst into the pail, he could drown in a matter of minutes (three, to be exact). If you use the type with a deodorizer cake, your baby could fish it out and eat it. (And like most deodorizing products, they're toxic.)

If you use disposable diapers, I highly recommend a pail in the style of the Diaper Genie. This handy little gizmo is too small for your child to fall into, and requires no deodorizers. It wraps each individual diaper in a sheath of plastic to keep out the smell. It's easy to put diapers in, but special latches keep kids from taking the diapers, or the hazardous plastic, out.

If you must use a traditional diaper pail, find one with a latch too complicated for your child to open, and keep it locked at all times.

Top bunks

If you have more than one child who's flown the crib, you may have decided on bunk beds as a way to economize your space. But be aware that beds with more than three inches of space between the headboard and the frame of the bed, and those with decorative cutouts in the head- or footboards pose a strangulation risk. More than twenty-six children since 1990 have died when their heads became caught between the headboard and frame, according to the CPSC. Thousands of bunk beds have been recalled for this reason.

Falling mattresses or foundations can also seriously injure or kill a small child, and mattresses and/or foundations that rest only on ledges are unsafe. They need additional supports, such as wood slats, metal straps, or sturdy wires, to hold them in place.

If you have an unsafe bunk bed that needs mattress support, write to Bunk Bed Kit, P.O. Box 2436, High Point, NC 27261 for a free cross-wire support kit you can use to repair the bed.

Also go over your bunk bed thoroughly (the way you would a crib) to make sure there are no loose, broken, or missing parts.

Toy chests

If you've solved your toy-storage dilemma with a toy chest, make sure it's a safe one. Children have been severely injured or killed when heavy lids have fallen closed on them, or they have become trapped inside toy boxes.

If the heavy lid of your toy box falls on your child while he is trying to lift it (or your toddler is using the open box to pull herself up), it could cause a concussion or trap his neck between the lid and the edge of the toy chest.

A child who crawls inside the chest to hide could become trapped and suffocate if the lid falls closed.

If you are buying a new toy chest, the Consumer Product Safety

Commission recommends looking for one that uses a support to hold the hinged lid open in any position in which it is placed, or one with a detachable lid. The chest should also have ventilation holes that won't be blocked when you stand it next to a wall. The lid of your child's toy chest should never have a latch.

If you already have a toy chest with a hinged lid, you should either buy a spring-loaded lid-support device that helps hold the lid open, or remove the lid completely. If the chest does not have airholes, it's a good idea to cut or drill some, sanding everything smooth when you are finished.

Other furnishings

Any piece of large furniture in your child's room that is top-heavy is cause for concern. Some dressers are big enough to tip over and crush a small child. If you have a heavy dresser you want to use in your child's room, consider filling the bottom drawers with bricks, books, or other heavy objects to keep it from tipping over if your child decides to climb on it (inevitable). Also make sure drawer knobs and handles are securely fastened so they don't break while your child is climbing. (And of course it never hurts to teach your child *not* to climb on the furniture.)

Extras

- Any paint used in your child's room should be free of lead, a dangerous metal that can poison the system and cause irreversible brain damage. (See "Lead.")
- Cover exposed outlets, or place heavy pieces of furniture in front of them. (See "Electrical Outlets.")
- Night-lights can start fires if they come in contact with pillows, blankets, or other flammable materials. To avoid this, plug in night-lights as far away from your child's bed as possible. Or

choose a night-light with a cooler, mini–neon bulb, rather than the traditional four- or seven-watt bulb.

- Every month, a child is strangled on a window cord. If your child's windows have curtains or blinds with long cords or drawstrings, shorten the strings or tie them up to keep them out of your child's reach. (A clothespin is handy for this.) (See "Windows.")
- If your child's room is above the ground floor, secure the windows with bars or locks to prevent falls. Never place furniture that would allow your child to climb up to the window near the window, and don't rely on screens to hold your child in. (See "Windows.")
- Peel off and throw away labels and decals from products in your child's room if she is likely to put them in her mouth (usually ages three or four and under). They are a choking hazard.

Resources

"Safety Shower," Associated Press news bulletin, February 29, 1996.

"Tips for Your Baby's Safety," "Your Used Crib Could Be Deadly," "CPSC Bans Infant Cushions: Safety Alert," "Infants Can Choke on Plastic Decals from Baby Walkers and Other Products," "Each Year, More Children Die in Home Accidents Than from All Childhood Diseases Combined," "Warning! Fire Hazard with Nightlights," "CPSC Warns of Strangulation with Crib Toys," "Furniture Can Tip Over on Children," "CPSC Warns Consumers of Bunk Bed Entrapment Hazard and Mattress Support Collapse," "Baby Product Safety Tips," *The Safe Nursery,* "CPSC Warns Parents About Infant Strangulation Caused by Failure of Crib Hardware," "Some Crib Cornerposts May Be Dangerous," "CPSC Warns That Tubular Metal Bunk Beds May Collapse," and "Soft Bedding Products and Sleep Position Contribute to Infant Suffocation Deaths," from the U.S. Consumer Product Safety Commission; (800) 638-2772.

"Safe and Sound for Baby: A Guide to Baby-Product Safety, Use and Selection," from the Juvenile Products Manufacturers Association, 2 Greentree Centre, Box 955, Marlton, NJ 08053.

CHRISTMAS

So this is Christmas, and a lot of injuries seem to go with the merriment—especially for kids.

Failure Analysis Associates, a consulting firm that investigates injuries, accidents, and natural disasters, reports that emergency-room visits for children under age two more than double during the two weeks before Christmas and remain high throughout the holiday season. Among six- and seven-year-olds, the number of visits also takes a jump at yuletide, and even adults are prone to about a 30 percent increase in injuries at this time of year.

The main factor seems to be the stress that accompanies our holiday cheer. We've got lots to do, and we simply don't pay as much attention to keeping our kids as safe as we should.

A large portion of kids' injuries around the end of December are caused by toys. That wouldn't surprise most people given the time of year, but the toys doing the damage aren't from this year's Santa bag. "It isn't the new toys coming into the house that raise the toy injury rate," says Dr. Christine Wood of Failure Analysis Associates, who attributes the injuries to child boredom and lack of parental supervision.

Crib-related injuries also take a big jump around Christmas/ Hanukkah. "It seems like parents may be putting kids in their cribs in a frantic attempt to get some things done," says Dr. Wood, adding that television-set-related injuries (cuts, bruises) also increase. "The things that you're trying to use to entertain them and keep them contained become the hazards."

Wood suggests using nursery monitors (even if your kids are older) to help you keep tabs on the children while you are in another room attending to holiday cooking or gift-wrapping chores that can't wait and are best accomplished solo. By the way, take care not to leave the scissors, tape, and other gift-wrapping tools within reach.

But there will be occasions when you have no choice but to

abandon the task at hand and spend some time on parent detail. "Sometimes you may just need to take them to the park or something and let them play," says Wood. It may even help reduce your own stress level (remember that jump in adult injuries).

Decking the halls

Most of us know enough to put the ceramic Santa out of reach on the mantel. And we carefully arrange our tree so that the hand-blown glass icicles are up top, while the wooden angels adorn the bottom. Maybe that's why *Christmas-tree lights* are the biggest decorating danger, accounting for about half of all ornament injuries. And most of these are not electrical burns (though these do happen), according to Wood.

It seems the tiny twinklers look like candy to kids, who put them in their mouths, bite down, and either swallow the broken pieces or are cut by the broken lights. Thermal burns (from lights that get hot) are also a problem. To protect your children from Christmas-tree injury:

- Try a smaller tree placed up on a table.
- Put lights only halfway down your tree.
- Put breakable ornaments up high, or don't use them.

If your tree isn't your only living decoration, keep in mind that poinsettia and holly are poisonous. U.S. poison-control centers get about ninety-two thousand calls about plant poisonings in children under age six each year, and the numbers are invariably higher at Christmas. Mistletoe is also dangerous, but is usually hung up so high the kids can't reach it (just make sure it stays above the door). (See "Plants.")

We also like to decorate ourselves around the holidays, and that means a rise in jewelry-related injuries, says Wood. These injuries include jewelry swallowed by children as well as jewelry stuck up noses, in ears, etc. So remember to put your jewelry away after that party, and don't give jewelry to children too young to wear it safely—no matter how special the occasion.

Decking the malls

No family can get through the holidays without major shopping. So it's no surprise that kids get hurt during the course of holiday purchasing.

"You've got a lot more people out there shopping," says Wood, and that means more crowded parking lots, lots of other people with frazzled nerves, stress—in short, multiple distractions that can take your attention away from your children, who are themselves a distraction. "When you're trying to get a certain number of tasks accomplished and watch a child at the same time, it becomes difficult," says Wood.

Planning ahead and allowing a little extra time to get things done is almost sure to yield a safer shopping experience. Shopping early is one way to reduce your time in the holiday crowds; shopping by catalog is another.

But even the most efficient holiday planner may end up with two or three more errands to run on the Saturday before Christmas when the kids have skipped their nap and you haven't had time to fix lunch yet. In this case, Wood advises that you make your trip as efficient as possible. Know what you plan to get, and call stores ahead to make sure they have it in stock. (See "Shopping—Stores and Malls.")

Travel

Holiday shopping and visiting mean more time in the car and more traffic on the roads, so you need to be more careful than usual about car safety. You may end up getting your child in and out of the car seat more often than normal, and you still need to be careful every time, even if you have an armload of packages and three more stores to visit.

And stow those packages carefully. They can become loose objects that get bounced around the car and injure passengers. The trunk is the best place for your holiday purchases. (See "Car Safety.")

When you get to Grandma's house, or wherever your holiday destination may be, take a moment to scout out the terrain and make sure your children will have a safe visit. (See "Visiting.")

Cheers

You won't have much to celebrate if you have to leave a holiday party early with an injured child. These injuries often happen while parents are distracted by the spirit or the spirits of the occasion. Whether you are the guest or host, do as much childproofing as is practical, and make sure someone is watching the kids. (See "Parties [grown-up].")

Too many cooks

The number of burns and scalds increases at holiday time because holiday cooking and baking are often mixed with socializing. Wood says injuries to adults rise along with those to children because cooking in this type of environment with its many distractions can be dangerous.

Your best bet at staying safe in the kitchen is to exercise a little control over your environment, says Wood. This means there are certain times when you'll just have to keep the kids out of the room. (See "Kitchen.")

Big bird

Your turkey-and-dressing recipe may have been handed down from your great-grandmother, but that doesn't mean you have her experience in safely preparing the big bird.

A fresh turkey should be bought no more than a day or two before the feast, according to the National Safety Council, but frozen birds (provided they are kept frozen) can be purchased months in advance. It is best to thaw your frozen friend in the refrigerator, allowing one day of thawing for every five pounds of bird. If you've run out of time or not planned ahead, scrub the sink, secure Tom in a heavy freezer bag, and submerge in cold water. Change the water every thirty minutes, and allow thirty minutes of thawing time per pound. Cook the bird as soon as it has thawed.

Stuffing should be cooked separately from the turkey, according to the Los Angeles County Health Department, while the National Safety Council says it's okay to stuff the bird just before you put it in the oven. Either way, turkey should be cooked to an internal temperature of 180 degrees Fahrenheit, and served within thirty minutes of cooking.

Leftovers should be refrigerated as soon as dinner is over. Meat can be kept safely for four days, while leftover stuffing and gravy will last only two.

Resources

Failure Analysis Associates, Inc; (415) 326-9400.

"Food Safety Tips for Holiday Feasts," from the California Department of Health Services.

"Seasonal Stress," "Stranded in the Snow," "Holiday Turkey Safety," "Your Safe and Festive Tree," from the National Safety Council, 1121 Spring Lake Dr., Itasca, IL 60143-3201.

USDA Meat and Poultry Hotline; (800) 535-4555.

CLOTHING

You may think of your child's clothes in many ways—already too small, permanently stained, I thought we threw that away. . . . But most fashion statements are not likely to do permanent damage. The following just might:

- **Drawstrings** on jackets, sweatshirts, hooded T-shirts, etc. can catch on anything from crib posts to playground equipment to school-bus doors. Seventeen children were killed this way between January 1985 and September 1995, and another forty-two were injured.

  In well over half the accidents, drawstrings around the hoods or necks of children ages two to eight caught on playground equipment. Usually, the string got stuck on the guardrail at the top of the slide, and strangled the child when he slid down. One four-year-old girl was strangled while climbing over a fence.

  The rest of the deaths and injuries were caused by drawstrings at children's waists catching in the handrail of the school bus or in the door. When the bus drove away, the child was dragged along and sometimes run over by the bus. These kids were generally seven to fourteen years old.

  The Consumer Product Safety Comission warns parents against buying shirts with drawstrings at the neck or waist for their children. If your child already has shirts, jackets, or sweatshirts with drawstrings at the hood or neck, remove them completely.

  Drawstrings at the waists of clothing should be shortened so that no more than three inches is hanging outside the garment at either end. The drawstring should also be sewn to the shirt in the middle so that it cannot be pulled out through one side and become long enough to catch on something. Parents should also remove toggles or knots from the ends of the drawstrings.

- **Loose clothing**, such as scarves, ponchos, attached mittens, and hoods can also catch on playground equipment and strangle children, or cause them to trip and fall. Look your child over before she goes out to play, and make sure there's nothing trailing.
- **Necklaces or bibs** can catch on cribs, doorknobs, or other furniture and strangle your baby. Save the necklaces for when your child is older (they could also be broken and lost, or end up being swallowed). Take off your baby's bib immediately after feeding, or use a bib that attaches with Velcro fasteners, which will come apart if the bib catches on something. *Never* tie a pacifier, toy, or any other object around your baby's neck.
- **Buttons**, **bows** or any small decorations that can pull loose from a baby or toddler's clothing are choking hazards. Avoid them until your child is old enough that you're sure she won't swallow them. No matter how securely the object appears to be sewn, your toddler's amazing little hands can no doubt pull it loose.
- **Socks** are slippery, and letting children run around in them is bad for both sock and child. The socks get even dirtier than usual, and the child is more likely to slip and fall. Try soft slippers with rubberized bottoms instead.
- **Shoelaces** that don't stay tied are a fall waiting to happen, as well as a minor frustration. I've had the most luck with what I call the Mommy Knot. Tie a bow as usual, then tie the loops into a knot. The laces won't come untied, but are easy to get undone when you're ready.
- **Zippers** can catch the skin of an unexperienced dresser. While this is certainly no life-threatening hazard, it often becomes a minor emergency because the parent isn't sure how to get the skin loose—especially if the child is a boy and the skin caught in the zipper is his . . . well, you get the idea. *Pediatrics for Parents* recommends cutting the zipper off at the bottom, causing it to fall apart and release the trapped skin.

Resources

"Zippered In," *Pediatrics for Parents,* volume 16, number 4.

"Strings, Cords, and Necklaces Can Strangle Infants," "Strings Can Strangle Children on Playground Equipment," "Guideline for Drawstrings on Children's Outerwear," and "CPSC Works with Industry to Remove Drawstring Hazard," from the U.S. Consumer Product Safety Commission; (800) 638-2772.

COMPUTERS

When you plugged your computer into a modem, you invited a whole new world into your home, and you may rightly suspect that it contains some hazards you don't yet understand. To make matters worse, your child may be a skilled surfer of the Net, pushing out ahead of you to explore on her own. But don't be daunted by this parallel universe. All the parenting skills you use in the real world apply on-line, and the general principles that guided you through making your child's nursery safe will help you avoid the dangers of cyberspace. Just use your common sense, and you can make the Internet as safe a place for your child to play as your own backyard.

There are two main hazards to address in cyberspace. The first is the questionable material—namely pornography and graphic violence—that is readily accessible. The second is that your child could use on-line services to arrange a face-to-face meeting with someone and risk his or her safety.

Questionable material

Currently several hundred Internet newsgroups contain sexually explicit material, and numerous sites on the World Wide Web offer pictures and written material depicting sexual situations, according to the makers of SurfWatch, software made to help block access to this material. If you subscribe to an on-line service such as America On-line, Prodigy, or CompuServe, your service provider may offer software to block your child's access to pornographic and violent materials, and to chat groups where adult topics may be discussed. America On-line offers SurfWatch technology free to its subscribers with Macintosh systems and PCs to help them limit access to materials and sites on the Web. It is also available directly to consumers, with monthly updates to block new sites. You can reach SurfWatch at (800) 458-6600, or check out your local software retailer for similar products. Just remember that you have to employ these devices for them to work, and as your child becomes more skilled at the computer, he or she may be able to find ways around them. Also keep in mind that this software can't block out individual users trying to contact your child.

Questionable characters

"The Internet is unique in its ability to guarantee anonymity," says Steve Winshell, owner of the Evolution Center, a computer training center for children. This means that the person your child is "chatting with" may not be who they say they are. Someone claiming to be a twelve-year-old girl might actually be a forty-year-old man, so on-line friendships must be approached with extreme caution.

Lawrence J. Magid, a syndicated columnist and author of "Child Safety on the Information Highway," a pamphlet copublished by the National Center for Missing and Exploited Children, recommends a few simple family rules to ensure your child's on-line encounters are safe:

• Never give out your address, telephone number, or school name on a public chat or bulletin board; think twice before giving your age, marital status, or financial information, and consider using a pseudonym or unlisting your child's name if your service allows it.

- Never let your child arrange a face-to-face meeting with someone they've met on-line without parental supervision.
- Never respond to obscene or belligerent bulletin-board messages. Encourage your children to tell you when they receive a message via the computer that makes them uncomfortable, and report these incidents to your service provider.

But the best way of all for you to guarantee safety in your child's on-line environment is for you to spend a little time there yourself. Consider moving the computer into the family room or another room where the family gathers. "If the parent is in the room, they're going to know what is going on," says Winshell, because everything comes up on-screen. This means your child can't view or download pornographic or violent materials, or have an X-rated chat without your knowledge.

Magid advises parents to talk to their children if they become concerned about the child's on-line activities, and to seek the advice of other computer users. Knowledge is power, so get to know the territory. If you don't know how to log on to the service, have your child show you. You wouldn't send your child to a new school or playground you had never visited, nor would you send him off to play with a friend you had never met. So get to know your child's on-line friends and the electronic "neighborhood" where they meet.

Resources

"Child Safety on the Information Highway," by Laurence J. Magid. Available through the National Center for Missing and Exploited Children. (800) 843-5678.

DIAPERING

A newborn needs changing about a dozen times a day, so the location and the tools you choose for these daily changes are easily as important as deciding between cloth and disposables. The Juvenile Products Manufacturers Association recommends selecting a sturdy table equipped with straps that will restrain your baby when you are changing or dressing her—or purchasing a strap separately and installing it yourself. I do not.

Falls from changing tables result in several deaths and countless injuries every year. Even the sturdiest straps are sometimes left unfastened, and as your baby grows, her strength will amaze you. Don't let that surprise end in tragedy when your curious toddler finally masters the safety latch and tumbles off the table.

If you don't perch your baby on a high table, he can't fall off, so arm yourself with a plastic or rubberized changing mat that allows you to change your child either in his crib, where the high sides prevent him from falling out, or on the floor. This method is safest, and will save you the trouble and expense of buying a piece of furniture you will only use for a year or two. If changing your baby in the crib hurts your back, try the couch, or even your own bed. The potential drop is still a lot shorter than the drop from most changing tables.

If you feel you must use a changing table, or if your day-care provider uses one, make sure your child is securely strapped in *every single time,* and have all diapering necessities at hand so you are never more than an arm's length from the baby. New types of changing mats—one with stiff foam sides and another that is V-shaped, creating a "valley" that keeps your baby from rolling—will help prevent accidents in babies too young to crawl. No type of strap or padding is guaranteed to stop a crawler or toddler from trying to climb off the table. They really are best changed on the floor.

Changes

Diaper wipes, baby powders, and some treatments for diaper rash can be irritating and even hazardous to your baby. Here is the bottom line concerning which products to avoid and what to use instead.

Baby powder of any kind should be avoided because the fine dust it generates usually finds its way into your baby's lungs, where it can cause severe coughing and even life-threatening choking. The talcum variety is often contaminated with asbestos fibers, which can cause pneumonia or chronic lung disease if your baby breathes them on a regular basis. Cornstarch, the alternative to talc, is not much better because it can encourage the growth of germs that cause diaper rash. No powder of any kind is really necessary if you take the time to make sure your baby's bottom is dry (either air-dried or with a towel) before putting on a fresh diaper.

Diaper wipes may contain alcohol and other chemicals that irritate baby's sensitive skin—especially skin already sore from diaper rash. (They're also cold on the bottom, which most babies hate.) An excellent alternative is to fill a new spray bottle with a mixture of one tablespoon of baking soda for every four ounces of springwater. Use this to rinse your baby's bottom with each diaper change. The alkalinity of the baking soda helps neutralize the acid content of urine and stool, preventing diaper rash. For the big messes, try a warm, wet washcloth or paper towel first, or simply rinse your baby's diaper area under a warm running tap. When you're on the go, keep a wet washcloth in a Ziploc bag in the diaper bag, along with some paper towels. (Note: Diaper wipes moistened with witch hazel are less irritating than traditional wipes when you need to use them.)

Prescription diaper rash creams, such as Mycolog, Mytrex, and Lotrisone, contain potent steroids that can produce loss of skin pigmentation, itching and burning, atrophy or thinning of the skin, permanent stretch marks, suppression of the adrenal glands, and headaches. Your doctor should only prescribe these medications as a last resort for severe diaper rash.

Resources

The Natural Nursery: The Parent's Guide to Ecologically Sound, Nontoxic, Safe, and Healthy Baby Care by Louis Pottkotter, M.D. FAAP (Contemporary Books, 1994).

Smart Medicine for a Healthier Child, by Janet Zand, LAc, OMD, Rachel Walton, RN, and Bob Rountree, M.D. (Avery, 1994).

"Baby Product Safety Tips," from the U.S. Consumer Product Safety Commission; (800) 638-2772.

DISASTERS

My daughter experienced her first natural disaster, an earthquake, at five months of age. Fortunately, it was only a 6.0, but as we huddled in the doorway at four A.M. in various stages of undress, I realized we were completely unprepared. Lauren slept through the whole thing, but I lost many nights of sleep over what *might* have happened.

Be prepared

The best way to protect your children from harm in the event of a disaster is to be prepared for one yourself.

Do your homework by learning which disasters are most possible for the area where you live and how to prepare for them. You can get this information from your local American Red Cross chapter.

Next, discuss openly with your family—children included— what types of disasters might hit your area and what would happen if they did. Would your home lose power, water, and gas? Would you have to evacuate or find someplace to take cover (as during an earthquake or severe storm)? Would you know the disaster was coming? How can your family deal with each of the possible consequences?

Sharing this information with your children will protect them in case of an emergency, and make them feel safer knowing your family is ready for whatever trouble may come. "It's important for children to have a sense of control [in a disaster] just like it is for adults," says Perry Zinberg, Ph.D., a child psychologist with Children's Hospital of Orange County, California, "and the way you do that is to have a plan. They're likely to feel less anxiety if they know what to do."

The plan

Family disaster plans vary depending on the family and what that family is preparing for. But the basic components are the same.

Start by figuring out how you would ride out the disaster itself—taking cover, finding shelter, or evacuating. Those in earthquake country should find the best location to ride out a quake in each room (e.g., under a heavy table, in a secure doorway). Those in storm terrain should have a storm cellar. And *everyone* should plan at least two exits out of every room in case of fire. Having your children help you draw a floor plan of the house indicating all possible shelters is a fun way to help the whole family remember this important information.

If you have children young enough to need your help getting to safety, make sure you designate an adult to assist each child so there is no confusion. Be clear in telling the child who will come to help them, and what they should do if no one is able to come.

Establish meeting places inside and outside your home, and outside your neighborhood in case the family becomes separated.

This is especially important to the children, because one of their biggest fears is being separated from their parents or left alone.

Learn what to do in the event your family is evacuated, and plan a list of things you can take with you. Don't forget to make provisions for your pets.

This is also a good time to discuss the disaster plans in place at your child's school or day-care center. Make sure the kids know who can make a telephone call for them if a disaster strikes while they are at school, and how they will be reunited with you. Your child should have a personal disaster kit at school, including a family photo for security.

Since it is often difficult to make local calls in an area hit by a disaster, make sure everyone in the family (and your child's school) has the number of an out-of-state friend or relative you can all call if you become separated. This person can act as a communication link until the family is back together.

When you've worked out all the details, write the plan down so that everyone remembers it, but keep in mind that this won't be enough for the kids. Practicing your plan by having disaster drills will help store it in everyone's long-term memory. (And the kids might even think it's fun.) The North Carolina Cooperative Extension Service recommends holding family drills every six months. These are a good time to review the plan and make sure it is still a good fit.

Everyone who is old enough should know how to call 911 for help (See "Telephone"), and where to find the water, gas, and electricity shutoffs. Older children can even learn how to turn the utilities off. It's also a good idea if *at least* one person in the family learns CPR and basic first aid.

The stash

The American Red Cross warns families that they'll probably be on their own for at least three days in the event of a disaster and should plan accordingly. This means having the necessary supplies on hand at home and in the car (since disasters don't always wait until you get home).

All your family really needs to survive is food, water, and shelter, and this is where you should concentrate your supply efforts. Everything else you store is solely for comfort, but the more comfortable you can keep your children, the safer they will feel. At an absolute minimum, you should have:

- Three gallons of water per person, replaced with fresh every three months. "Remember that hydration is more important for kids," says Ross Miller, M.D., of Children's Hospital Los Angeles, so add juice and electrolyte solution such as RiceLyte to your stock. For infants, keep a supply of powdered formula and bottles stashed away. (If you are nursing, keep in mind that your body will run out of milk if you don't store adequate food and water for yourself.) For toddlers and older children who demand their glass of milk, consider storing long-life milk.
- Three cans of food per person, per day for a week. It sounds like a lot, but you can build a supply quickly if you buy one extra of each type of canned food you purchase, and put the date on the top with a permanent marker. When it's been there for six months, rotate it into your regular kitchen stock and replace it with a new can. And don't forget to stash away a manual can opener!
- Some type of tent, and plenty of wool blankets or sleeping bags for everyone in the family. These could be the supplies you already use for family camping trips.
- A change of clothes for everyone in the family. This should include extra hats for any child under the age of two, because children lose a lot of heat through their heads, according to Miller. The younger the child, the more important it is to have a hat.
- A first-aid kit, to which you should add children's Tylenol and a medicine dropper, says Miller. Also store other medicines that are familiar to your child. "Have whatever you normally use [for

treating cuts and scrapes] on hand, because children [can be] frightened by unfamiliar things," says Zinberg.

- Anything special that family members might need, such as prescription medications, or an extra pair of glasses.

Children may require a few extra comforts:

- Travel games, coloring books or other toys, and a cuddly stuffed animal to hang on to (in case you're not able to rescue their regular "woobie"). "The first thing you want to do with most children is grab their favorite transitional object, because they may have to leave their house and sleep in a different place. [At my house] we packed a little bag with all my kids' favorite things," says Miller, adding his children's "earthquake suitcases" contain age-appropriate toys, crayons, and snacks— "the few items you would take if you're going to visit Grandma. I think it keeps their mind off some of the fear that's definitely there," he adds.

Another item Miller suggests packing for each child is a disposable plastic light stick, because, "they're great for security, and they make a cool little flashlight."

There are plenty of other things you can store that will help make riding out a disaster more bearable. Exhaustive lists are available from the Red Cross or by calling the Emergency Preparedness Information Center. Don't count on being able to buy these things after the disaster hits. Stores may not be able to open if they are damaged, or if power outages keep their cash registers from operating. And even if stores are open, there will be plenty of other people trying to buy what few items are available.

Aftershocks

The days and weeks following a disaster can be as frightening to children as the disaster itself. They've been scared by what has happened, their routines are disrupted, and their house may have been damaged or destroyed.

One of the most important things you can do for any child who has been through a disaster is to reestablish as much of the normal order of things as possible, as quickly as possible. Even if you are spending the night in an emergency shelter or camped out in your backyard, don't skip that bedtime story. Try to salvage normal mealtimes. Brush their teeth. These little things give children hope that things will eventually get back to normal.

According to FEMA and the Red Cross, children are most afraid that

- the event will happen again.
- someone will be injured or killed.
- they will be separated from family.
- they will be left alone.

To combat these fears, keep the family together as much as possible. Calmly tell the children everything you know about what has happened, and what will happen in the immediate future. Encourage them to talk about the disaster and about their fears. And to give them a sense of control over their situation, include them in cleanup activities.

Children react to stress in different ways, but the most common indicator that a child is traumatized following a disaster is unusual changes in behavior or appearance. Children under age seven are more likely to exhibit regressive behavior (thumb sucking, loss of toilet training, separation anxiety, increased whining and dependency), while older children are more likely to act out or conversely, withdraw.

Other signs of distress:

- disaster-related fears
- trouble sleeping

- apathy
- looking sad or depressed
- complaints of headache, stomachache, or other illnesses
- aggression, disobedience, destructiveness
- irritability, sudden mood swings
- lethargy, fatigue

Your child may need additional help coping if these symptoms persist for more than two weeks, if several different symptoms are present at once, or if your child threatens to or tries to harm himself.

Resources

The North Carolina Cooperative Extension Service offers a terrific natural disaster program for families, which I accessed through their Web site at http://www.ces.ncsu.edu/disaster.

"Your Family Disaster Plan," and "Helping Children Cope with Disaster," from the American Red Cross and the Federal Emergency Management Agency.

"How to Prepare for an Emergency" from the Emergency Preparedness Information Center, Seattle, WA; (206) 937-5658. http://www.theepicenter. com.

"Children, Stress, and Natural Disasters," from the University of Illinois at Champaign-Urbana Cooperative Extension Service Disaster Resource; (217) 333-2912.

DOORS

There are two basic threats a door poses to a child. If the door has a lock, the child can lock herself in a room—and not necessarily be able to get out again. If the child, or anyone else, is opening and closing the door, her fingers can get pinched in the doorjamb—usually near the hinges. There are a number of ways you can shut the door on these accidents:

To prevent lock-ins:

Take the locking knobs off your inside doors. This is a surefire way to keep the kids from locking themselves in a room. However, it requires buying new doorknobs, and you may want those doors to lock again someday.

Put tape across the latch. This will prevent the door from locking by keeping it from latching tight. As long as the kids don't decide to peel off the tape, you're okay. (This is also a great temporary fix for locking doors at the homes of friends and relatives you're visiting.)

Keep the door locked so the child can't get into the room in question. This will work as long as you don't mind the inconvenience, and can remember *always* to lock the door. Just keep in mind that the one time you forget, your child will almost certainly find his way into that room.

Buy one of those gadgets that keeps your child from turning the doorknob. These are kind of like childproof caps for doors. The trouble with these is that children may quickly learn to use them, while adults find them too frustrating to operate. And they don't work at all if someone leaves the door open.

In a pinch:

Install a gadget that keeps your door from closing all the way. This will keep the kids' hands from getting crushed, but may also frustrate you when you decide you really do need to close that door.

Drape a towel across the top of the door. This will also keep the door from closing, but is easily removed—which could be a problem if the towel falls off.

Try an over-the-door hook thick enough to keep the door from closing. It will stay on better than a towel, but is still easily removed.

And it gives you a place to hang towels, bathrobes, etc. If the one you buy isn't thick enough, you can probably make it work by wrapping it with masking tape.

To stop chokings: Replace metal doorstops that have a rubber cap with newer, one-piece models.

EASTER

Scrambling to get ready for spring? Here are a few simple safety tips that were too good to hide.

Your egg is cooked

Whether the chicken or the egg came first, no one knows, but both can be dangerous when undercooked. *Salmonella enteritidis,* a type of bacteria associated with food poisoning, can cause diarrhea, fever, and abdominal pain lasting five to seven days. The illness can be life threatening in infants, but is easily avoided with a few simple precautions. These include never using eggs with cracked shells, and never eating undercooked eggs. (See "Food.")

To properly hard-boil eggs, put them in a single layer in the bottom of a saucepan. Add enough water to cover the eggs by at least an inch, and bring quickly to a boil over high heat. Boil the eggs for at least seven minutes, then remove from the heat and run cold water over the eggs until they are completely cooled. Store cooled eggs in their cartons in the refrigerator (at a temperature of forty-five degrees or colder) until you are ready to color them.

Never boil or color cracked eggs.

True colors

When choosing a commercial egg-coloring kit, keep the ages of your children in mind. There are plenty of cool kits out there containing everything from glitter to markers. Most are completely nontoxic, so the eggs will be safe to eat. Just make sure the kit doesn't have small parts that will end up in the mouth of a toddler.

For the ultimate nontoxic dye solutions, the American Egg Board recommends adding any of the following to a cup of boiling water and a tablespoon of vinegar:

fresh beets, cranberries, radishes or frozen raspberries: pink
yellow onion skins: orange
ground turmeric: yellow
spinach leaves: green
canned blueberries or red cabbage leaves: blue

To avoid mess and hassle for smaller children, Dad or Mom can color the eggs first, then let the kids apply the stickers of their choice to add pizzazz.

Dye, dry, and return the eggs to their cartons in the refrigerator as quickly as you can. Eggs being decorated for a holiday display that will be kept out of the refrigerator should not be eaten.

Remember not to hide eggs too long before the hunt. When all are found, discard any that are cracked or have been out of the refrigerator for more than two hours. Post-Easter eggs kept in the refrigerator should be used within one week.

A basket case

At no time of year do you see more candy shaped to be such a perfect fit in a child's windpipe. Small chocolate eggs, marshmallow chicks, jelly beans—all can stick in the throat like a cork in a bottle. If you're the sole basket planner, you can avoid these choke-sized candies in favor of, say, hollow chocolate rabbits or holiday M&M's.

If a doting grandma, aunt, or teacher provides part of the stash, storing the candy in question in a special candy jar will at least allow you to dole it out under proper supervision. This way, you can give out one piece of candy at a time while your child is sitting down and can concentrate on chewing—and you're there to make sure everything goes down okay. If the candy is soft, cut it into safer-sized pieces.

If you are including toys in your child's basket, make sure they are age-appropriate and safe. (See "Toys" and childproofing checklists.) Flopsy, Mopsy, and Cottontail shouldn't have eyes that will pull off, stuffing that comes unstuffed, or ribbons that might get wrapped around your child's neck instead of theirs.

Discard "Easter grass," as well as any plastic wrapping that covered anything in the basket, or the basket itself, immediately after your child digs in. Fifteen children a year choke to death on plastic, says the Consumer Product Safety Commission.

Resources

"Easy Easter Egg Preparation, Care and Handling," from the Ohio Egg Marketing Program and the American Egg Board; (614) 882-6111.

"Making the Most of Easter Eggs," from the California Egg Commission and the California Department of Health Services.

Los Angeles County Department of Health Services.

"Cook Eggs Properly for Safe Easter, State Health Director Advises," from the California Department of Health Services.

"Approximately 15 Children Die Each Year—Children Still Suffocate with Plastic Bags," from the U.S. Consumer Product Safety Commission; (800) 638-2772.

ELECTRICAL OUTLETS/CORDS

When we moved into our house, which was built in 1924, one of the first things we discovered was that there were hardly any electrical outlets. We had nowhere to plug in the coffeemaker, blow dryer, or television set. This caused some inconvenience, but also meant the house was safer for our daughter.

In most cases, children who are electrocuted in their homes have bitten into an electrical cord, which can create temperatures as high as 2,500 degrees. The majority of these injuries are burns to the mouth, according to the Los Angeles Department of Water and Power. Most of the victims are six to thirty-six months old.

Luckily, prevention here is simple and usually inexpensive.

One good overall protective measure you can take is to have a ground-fault circuit interrupter hardwired into your home's electrical system. You need an electrician for this, but it's well worth the effort. A GFCI cuts off the current if someone comes into contact with an outlet or exposed wire, and will usually prevent electrocutions. It will not, however, prevent painful electrical shocks and burns, so some other safety measures are in order.

Outlets

There are a variety of devices you can use to cover an exposed electrical outlet to keep curious little hands away. My favorite is a large and heavy piece of furniture, but this only works for outlets you never use.

Tape is a handy way to cover outlets you need access to, but it only works for the tiniest tots. Nothing keeps a two-year-old out for long. And you have to remember to replace the tape after you've used the outlet.

The same is true of the little plastic "plugs" that fit directly into the outlet. These are readily available and easy to use, but your child will eventually learn to pull them out, and they really hurt if you step on them in your bare feet.

I think the best type of outlet protector for forgetful parents with active kids is the spring-loaded type that replaces the entire outlet cover. These contain a sliding plastic piece you move aside before you can plug in an appliance. The piece snaps back into place as soon as the plug is removed, covering the slots in the outlet. They are available at most hardware stores, and are fairly easy to install.

Experts say you should unplug most appliances when they're not in use, and this is especially true if you have small children. Your children have probably watched you plug things in and will be anxious to test their own skills in this area. For appliances you do have to leave plugged in (the lamp, the television set, the answering machine), you should either obscure the outlet entirely with a heavy piece of furniture (making sure not to pinch the cord or plug against the wall), or buy an outlet plate with a cover that locks closed over the plugs. This keeps children from unplugging the appliance and playing with the outlet.

Cords

The best way to keep children from chewing on electrical cords is to keep the cords and the children apart. Wind up all excess cords and secure them with string, a rubber band, or a twist tie near the appliance. The remainder of the cord should stay out of traffic areas and hidden from view as much as possible. But you should never run appliance or extension cords under carpets, because this creates a fire hazard.

Instead, run the cord along the wall. You can cover exposed cords with special flexible hollow moldings, which are designed to hide the cord safely while protecting it from excess wear.

In your efforts to get cords out of the way, make sure you don't pinch them against furniture or walls, and avoid kinking, twisting, or binding cords, which causes excess wear.

Current rules

Since electrical outlets and cords are everywhere, just babyproofing against them is not enough. You also have to begin teaching your child to respect electricity from an early age.

Tell them they will be badly hurt if they chew on or play with cords, or put things into outlets. If your child is old enough to use electrical appliances without your supervision (not until at least age nine or ten), teach her to plug in and unplug appliances properly. She should never force a plug into an outlet where it will not fit, and she should remove plugs only by grasping the plug near the outlet, not by pulling on the cord.

Resources

"Electrical Fire Safety" and "Keeping Current on Electrical Fire Safety," from the National Fire Protection Association, Batterymarch Park, Quincy, MA 02269-9101.

"Child's Guide to Electric Safety," from the Los Angeles Department of Water and Power.

"Electrical Safety Indoors," from Southern California Edison.

"Electrical Injuries and Fire Hazards," from the Alisa Ann Ruch Burn Foundation; (800) 242-BURN.

EXERCISE EQUIPMENT

For children, anything and everything rates as exercise equipment. But it's becoming more and more common for parents to keep a machine or two around to help Mom and Dad stay fit. Unfortunately, this equipment can be dangerous in little hands.

The Consumer Product Safety Commission reported that 1,200 children's fingers were amputated when they got caught in the moving bike wheel or the chain and sprocket assembly between 1985 and 1989. And these figures don't include injuries to other parts of the body, or from other types of equipment—such as weight machines, stair climbers or treadmills.

Room with a view

You'll go a long way toward keeping your kids and your exercise equipment apart if you keep it out of their line of sight. Don't plop the equipment down in front of the TV in the family room and expect them not to touch it. If you can, find a more remote area for your daily workout—even if you have to relegate your viewing to the small black-and-white television in the guest room. But don't make this your entire safety plan. Even if you put a locked door between the kids and the equipment, you should only purchase exercise machines with appropriate safety features:

Exercise bikes should have all moving parts covered, including spokes and wind fans.

Treadmills should have an emergency stop feature, an automatic starting speed under 2 mph, and enclosed motor and wiring.

Stair climbers should have an automatic stop feature, and enclosed mechanical parts and wiring.

Ski machines should not have footpads that can slide off and injure the user or bystanders.

Weight machines should have shielded weight stacks that cannot catch or pinch clothing or body parts.

It's also a good idea to make sure any machine you purchase is made of high quality materials, and has a wide, stable base that will prevent it from toppling over if your child decides to go a-climbing. This is also true of racks for free weights. Make sure your child can't tip over the rack, or pull the weights down on herself. And be sure to put your free weights away after each use. Your child could hurt himself lifting them, or could drop them on a leg or foot or roll them off a table or bench and injure himself.

Rules

It doesn't hurt to teach your children that they can hurt themselves by playing with your exercise equipment. Explain how they could injure their backs by lifting a weight that is too heavy for them, or break a bone by dropping a weight on their foot or hand. Point out that the moving parts of a machine can pinch, and that they could fall off a machine that is too big for them. If the kids still want to get some exercise, get involved in other activities that are safer for their size.

Resources

Complete Home Fitness Handbook, edited by Edmund R. Burke.
"Prevent Finger Amputations to Children From Exercise Bikes, Safety Alert" from the U.S. Consumer Product Safety Commission.

FAMILY ROOM

I have a small scar above my right eye—a faint line, about an inch long, between my eyebrow and eyelid. Most people don't even notice it, so almost no one knows that when I was two years old, I fell into the sharp corner of the stereo in the living room and came within half an inch of losing an eye. My mom said there was lots of blood and squealing, but no stitches.

That happened a couple of decades ago, but accidents such as these are still common. And old-fashioned common sense is still the best way to prevent them. Start by taking a tour of the room at your child's level—whether that's crawling, toddling, or tearing through at a dead run. Check out your kid's path, and the hazards you find in it.

- Keep cords, including electrical cords, telephone cords, and window-blind or curtain cords (See "Windows") wound up and out of the way. These present both trip-and-fall and electrocution hazards. (See "Electrical Outlets.") But don't put electrical cords under the rug, where they might start a fire.
- Watch for wobbly furniture, especially if your child is just learning to walk and may look to that tipsy end table as a way of achieving verticality. If you absolutely can't retire these items, move them to a room where your child doesn't spend much time, or at least get them out of high-traffic areas. We had a wobbly set of end tables that migrated temporarily to our bedroom to serve as bedside tables.
- The same goes for furniture with sharp corners or edges. A number of products have been created to "cushion the blow," but I recommend these only as an additional protective measure. My daughter never noticed our glass-topped coffee table until she discovered how much fun it was to peel off (and chew on—creating another safety hazard) those little plastic corner guards.
- Rocking chairs (which could rock your child straight to the floor, headfirst) and older-model recliners (that might trap a child's head in the space between footrest and seat cushion or footrest and the floor) should be off-limits unless the kids are supervised.
- Batten down the area rugs, or move them out of the line of fire.
- Develop a habit (and teach your child to help you) of picking up toys and any other objects on the floor that could cause someone to trip.
- Bookcases and shelving units should be sturdy (no brick-and-board specials) and bolted to the wall to prevent them from tipping over if your little monkey decides to go for a climb. And

avoid putting forbidden objects your child really wants on high shelves in plain sight. You might as well lay out the climbing gear.

- That's not to say you shouldn't put breakables and other dangerous items (fireplace matches, small objects that present a choking hazard, pens and pencils) out of reach. Just make sure they are also out of sight.
- Be especially careful about leaving the TV remote where your child can reach it. Given enough time, she might be able to figure out how to get the batteries out, and could chew her way to a serious chemical burn.
- Have a liquor cabinet? Keep it locked. It takes only a few ounces of the stuff to cause fatal alcohol poisoning.

If it's your child's mode of travel that's the problem, you might want to correct that, too. Discourage running, jumping, and general roughhousing in the house and your kids will get hurt less often. Start young. "We don't run in the house, chairs are for sitting, not bouncing," and "that's a bookcase, not a staircase" should echo throughout their childhood.

When our daughter was almost two years old, I spotted her and her father playing in the bedroom, where he was letting her walk around on the bed. I reminded him that I never allowed Lauren to stand on any piece of furniture. "Oh, she'll be all right," he replied.

As the last word left his mouth Lauren tumbled off the side of the bed, rebounded off the night table, and landed, screaming, on the floor. My rule was never questioned again. Sometimes it's Mom and Dad who have to learn the hard way.

Resources

"Room-by-Room Childproofing Guide," by Mark D. Widome, M.D., FAAP, *Healthy Kids, Birth–3,* from the American Academy of Pediatrics.

Caring for Your Baby and Young Child: Birth to Age 5, Steven P. Shelov, M.D., FAAP, editor. American Academy of Pediatrics, Bantam, 1993.

"CPSC Warns Parents About Child Accidents in Recliner Chairs," from the U.S. Consumer Product Safety Commission; (800) 638-2772.

FIRE

If you've ever dreamed you were trapped in a burning building, imagine what a nightmare it would truly be if it included the voices of your children, calling out for help.

A survey released in February 1996 by the National Fire Protection Association showed that most Americans felt confident about fire safety in their own homes. But U.S. fire departments still respond to more than two million fires every year, according to the National Safe Kids Campaign. More than 960 children a year ages fourteen and under die in residential fires, and another 44,000 are injured. Nearly 70 percent of the deaths, and over half of the injuries, are to children under age four.

The risk to kids

Children generally have the good sense to be scared of a fire, but this fear is often what keeps them from getting out of the house. Instead of calling for help, a child may hide under the bed or in the closet, thinking this will protect him from the fire. The sound of a smoke detector going off or the appearance of a firefighter in full gear may also frighten a child into hiding.

If the fire happens at night, however, a child might not even wake up, because children are easily overcome by the smoke and toxic fumes. In fact, 77 percent of six-to-nine-year-olds and 54 percent of children ages five and under who die from home fires die while they are asleep.

Cause and effect

Most fires that kill children ages five and under (76 percent, according to the National Safe Kids Campaign) are started by kids playing with fire. Almost half of these fire deaths happen between eight A.M. and four P.M., when children are most likely to be left alone. The blaze usually starts in the bedroom or living room, where kids are left to play. Bedding, mattresses, or upholstered furniture is often the first thing to ignite.

Putting out fires

Inspect your house or apartment for those hot little objects that can spark a full-blown fire—especially if you leave your children home alone.

- Lighters or matches left where children can get to them—even if they have to stand on a chair to do it.
- Furniture, clothes, or anything piled too close to a fireplace, heater, or radiator.
- Electrical hazards like too many cords plugged into the same socket, cords under rugs, appliances with old or frayed cords, or old extension cords that could overheat.
- Flammable liquids stored inside the home.

And since many fires happen at night, make sure the whole family is sleeping in flame-retardant jammies, on mattresses that meet the Federal Mattress Flammability Standard (which means they were bought later than 1973).

Where there's smoke

Prevention aside, the single most important (and the easiest) thing you can do to protect your kids from fire is to buy and install smoke detectors on every level of your home—preferably near the bed-rooms. Ninety percent of the children killed in home fires are killed in homes without working smoke detectors—the operative word here being *working*.

The chances of dying in a fire are cut in half by a smoke detector, but yours does your family no good if it is broken, the batteries are dead, or if you disabled it following that unfortunate charred Sunday dinner last month. (Which is why it is best to install the detectors away from the kitchen.) The National Safe Kids Campaign reports that while 92 percent of U.S. homes had at least one smoke detector as of 1993, just 74 percent had *working* detectors. And the National Fire Protection Association survey found that only 55 percent of households had tested their detectors in the past month to make sure they were working.

Remember, if your house catches fire while you are asleep, the flames probably won't wake you or your children. The smoke spreads more quickly than the flames, so it will reach you first, rendering you unconscious in your sleep.

So here's what you should do:

- Install smoke detectors on every level of your home or apartment, especially in bedrooms. (Don't be cheap. They only cost ten dollars, so buy as many as you need.)
- Test all your detectors once a month to make sure they are working. (Doing it right after you pay the rent or mortgage will help you remember.)
- Replace the batteries at least once a year.

Your kids should know

Teaching your children a thing or two about fires will help them stay cool if there's a fire in your house.

Kids should know that fires are fast. A little fire can engulf a house in a matter of minutes, so they should call an adult and get out of the house right away if even the smallest fire starts.

Kids should know that fires are dark, and that they won't be able to see much, and may not be able to breathe very well.

Kids should know how to get out of a fire. This means getting down on the floor to avoid the smoke, covering their mouths and noses with a cloth or their hands, and crawling to the nearest exit. Kids should know to touch doors before opening them, and to use another exit if the door is warm. Kids should know that fires are hot, with temperatures reaching more than six hundred degrees. This means they should never try to escape the house through the flames.

Kids should know your family's disaster plan, including two available exits from every room and an outside meeting place. (See "Disasters.")

Kids should know never to go back into a burning building, *no matter what.*

Kids should know how to call 911 for help. (See "Telephone.")

Resources _____

Perhaps your best resource for fire-prevention information is your local fire department. Many will inspect your home for fire hazards free of charge. They also have fire safety information for kids and parents alike and often conduct fire station open houses, equipment demonstrations, and other programs for school-age children. Give them a call. They would be happy to work themselves right out of a job.

Safe Kids Are No Accident: A Fire Safety Booklet for Kids, "This Week, 25 Children Will Die From Fire," "How Fire-Safe Is Your Home?", and "Residential Fire Injury," from the National Safe Kids Campaign; (202) 884-4993.

"Household Tips for the Prevention of Burns," from the Alisa Ann Ruch Burn Foundation; (800) 242-BURN.

"Household Extension Cords Can Cause Fires," from the U.S. Consumer Product Safety Commission; (800) 638-8270.

FIREPLACE

Your picture of a cozy family-at-home scene probably involves a cheerful fire in the fireplace. But the reality is that children and fireplaces are not a safe combination. If there is a fire in the fireplace, both fire and child require close, constant supervision to guarantee safety.

More than six thousand people are sent to emergency rooms each year because of injuries associated with the use of a fireplace. The majority of these are minor, and involve cuts and bruises to adults handling fireplace equipment. But sadly, the most serious injuries are burns, and the victims of these are usually children.

Children are usually injured in fireplace accidents in one of four ways:

- Their clothing comes into contact with the flame, or with sparks from the flame, and catches fire.
- Sparks from the fire land on nearby flammable material and start a blaze in the room.
- Adults use flammable liquids to rekindle a dying fire, causing an explosion and fire.
- The fireplace isn't vented or maintained properly or material other than wood is burned, causing carbon-monoxide poisoning.

Additional hazards are created by the matches adults commonly keep handy for lighting the fireplace, and when children get their hands on the "key" used to turn on gas-burning fireplaces.

No sparks

To protect children's clothing and other materials in the room from catching fire, guard your fireplace with a sturdy screen made of metal or heat-tempered glass. The safest of these attach firmly to the floor in some way. Fireplace inserts that put a glass door between the family and the fire are another good option. Just keep in mind that these doors get hot when a fire is burning, and could burn your child.

A flame-retardant hearth rug protects your flooring from burn holes caused by escaping sparks, and provides an additional barrier between the fire and anything flammable.

If you have a wood or coal stove, make sure you have a heat-resistant stove board underneath it to protect the floor from heat and embers. Install it at least three feet from walls, and keep the area clear of anything flammable.

Back off

Even with the sturdiest of screens and rugs, families need to enforce distance rules when a fire is burning. This means at least three feet between the flames and anything you don't want burned. If you have a hearth rug, you can use it to set safe boundaries for your children. A "no kids on the rug" policy will keep everyone a good distance away—especially when an adult has the screen or insert open to tend the fire. It is also important to keep anything flammable (kerosene, cleaning products, hair spray, furniture, newspapers) well away from a burning fireplace.

What to burn

Only dry, seasoned wood or artificial logs made for fireplace use are safe to burn in your fireplace. Coal, charcoal, or Styrofoam packaging can produce deadly quantities of carbon monoxide.

Burning fragments of paper or trash can be carried up into your chimney, where they can cause a chimney or roof fire.

If you use artificial logs, be sure to read and follow the directions on the package. Artificial logs should never be stacked as if they were wood. This could cause an explosion.

Never use gasoline, kerosene, or lighter fluid to rekindle a dying fire. This could also cause an explosion that puts your whole house in flames.

Up the chimney

Have your "Santa port" inspected yearly to make sure it is in proper working order. The ventilation provided by your chimney keeps dangerous carbon-monoxide gas from building up in your home. (See "Carbon Monoxide.") Your inspector can also remove deposits of creosote and carbon that can build up and pose a fire hazard.

While a fire is burning, you should always keep the flue or damper open to prevent CO buildup.

Burning wisdom

Having a fireplace generally means having a supply of matches and lighters around to light it. But these can't be kept too handy if there are children in the house. Children as young as two have started fires with matches and lighters, so store them as if they were a dangerous weapon. And as soon as your child is old enough to understand, take every opportunity to explain that matches and lighters are dangerous. If they find matches or a lighter, kids should be taught to bring them to an adult immediately.

Another thing that needs to be kept well out of your child's reach is the "key" used to turn on a gas-burning fireplace. Children love to imitate Mommy and Daddy and might turn the gas on. Even if the gas doesn't ignite and cause a fire or explosion, the noxious fumes are dangerous.

Your child could also be hurt playing with fireplace tools, so make sure these are off-limits. And if you have a hearth that is raised above the level of the floor, it is a good idea to cover the corners with some sort of soft material. More than 7,500 children are sent to the emergency room each year when they trip and fall against the hearth.

Resources

Fires in Your Home: Prevention and Survival, "Fire Prevention All Over Your Home," "Heating Without Getting Burned," and "Match and Lighter Fire Safety," from the National Fire Protection Association, Batterymarch Park, Quincy, MA 02269-9101.

Fireplaces fact sheet from the U.S. Consumer Product Safety Commission; (800) 638-2666.

FIREWORKS

It was a tradition in our family. Every summer we went to my grandparents' house to celebrate the Fourth of July with a barbecue and a big display of home fireworks—my favorite part.

Until the year Grandpa almost set my cousin and me on fire.

We escaped unharmed (though the chenille beach robe we were huddled under suffered greatly), but about twelve thousand people a year aren't so lucky, according to the U.S. Consumer Product Safety Commission. Hence, this chapter is not intended to tell you how to use home fireworks safely, it is an attempt to persuade you not to use them at all.

Your children may look forward to their yearly opportunity to play with fire, but they are also the ones most likely to get hurt if something goes wrong. In fact, more than half of firework injuries involve children, according to the National Fire Protection Association.

Who gets burned

Most fireworks injuries—63 percent in 1994—are burns, and most of these are to the hands, fingers, eyes, and face. And keeping the kids out of the action doesn't keep them safe. The largest proportion of serious firework-related eye injuries reported to the CDC between 1990 and 1994 were to bystanders, while only 35 percent were to operators.

Children and fireworks both move very fast. When things go wrong, they go wrong so quickly that there isn't much you can do to prevent injuries, according to the NFPA. And even a child you think is watching from a safe distance can end up in the thick of things before you can stop him from getting hurt.

Safe and sane

Consumer fireworks have been completely banned in ten states (Arizona, Connecticut, Delaware, Georgia, Massachusetts, Minnesota, New Jersey, New York, Rhode Island, and Vermont), but the District of Columbia and thirty-two other states allow use of at least some types of fireworks. Six other states (Illinois, Iowa, Maine, Maryland, Ohio, and Pennsylvania) permit only sparklers and other novelties such as poppers, wheels, and snaps.

But don't think you're safe just because you are purchasing fireworks that are legal in your community. It was a completely legal Safe and Sane sparkler that just about ignited my cousin and me. And these same sparklers, permitted in roughly thirty-eight states, caused more than nine hundred injuries serious enough for a trip to the emergency room in 1994 alone. About three hundred of these injuries were to children four or younger.

And while about one fourth of the injuries cited by the NFPA involved illegal types of fireworks, nearly two thirds were caused by fireworks permitted under federal law.

The big guns

Large firecrackers caused more total injuries than any other type of fireworks, according to the National Electronic Injury Surveillance System of the Consumer Product Safety Commission. (These can also permanently damage a child's hearing. See "Noise.") These were followed by bottle rockets, Roman candles, and sparklers.

If you look at injuries serious enough to require a trip to the hospital, large firecrackers are again a clear danger, accounting for a whopping 44 percent. No other type of fireworks even comes close.

However, bottle rockets are the biggest danger to the eyes, says a CPSC study. Injuries are caused by children aiming or throwing the rockets at another person, product malfunction (including immediate explosion), and the rocket ricocheting off hard surfaces and hitting another person.

Playing with fire

The National Fire Protection Association, the CPSC, and the U.S. Centers for Disease Control recommend abandoning home fireworks and attending public fireworks displays instead. They are free in many communities, and the experts generally put on a better show than Dad or Grandpa can manage. Your local fire department should have a list of these as July approaches.

But if you have your heart set on a backyard display, at least pass on the bottle rockets, cherry bombs, M-80s, and other explosive devices.

When using other types of fireworks, wear protective eyewear, keep a source of water nearby, and read and follow all firework manufacturer's directions. Keep young children completely away from fireworks and supervise older children closely if you decide to let them light the fuse. If something doesn't work, don't pick it up and try to re-light it. Leave it on the ground, and douse it with water.

Resources

"Serious Eye Injuries Associated with Fireworks—United States, 1990-1994," *Morbidity and Mortality Weekly Report,* the U.S. Centers for Disease Control, June 23, 1995, volume 44, number 24.
"U.S. Fireworks Injuries Remain High," *NFPA Journal,* July/August 1995, pp. 61-66.

FIRST-AID KITS

When accidental injuries do happen, it is important to have the necessary supplies on hand. Your family first-aid kit should contain the following items:

- latex gloves (2 pair) to protect you from exposure to blood and bodily fluids if you have to help someone outside the family
- alcohol wipes or antiseptic for cleaning wounds
- moist towelettes
- soap
- Band-Aids in assorted sizes
- scissors for cutting bandages
- hypoallergenic adhesive tape for securing bandages
- 2-inch sterile gauze pads (4 to 6)
- 4-inch sterile gauze pads (4 to 6)
- 2-inch sterile roller bandages (3 rolls)
- 3-inch sterile roller bandages (3 rolls)
- triangular bandages (3)

- safety pins for securing bandages
- eye dressing
- tweezers for removing splinters
- needle
- thermometer
- tube of petroleum jelly or other lubricant
- tongue blades (2)
- cold pack
- first-aid handbook
- insect-sting preparation
- sunscreen
- aspirin or nonaspirin pain reliever
- antidiarrhea medication
- antacid for upset stomach
- syrup of ipecac to induce vomiting if advised by the poison control center
- laxative
- activated charcoal to use if advised by the poison control center
- poison-control-center telephone number
- any prescription medications members of your family might require (such as asthma inhalers or heart medication)

It is also a good idea to keep a scaled-down version of this kit in your car. You can buy a ready-made kit at most grocery and drug stores, or you can put one together yourself. This way, if you can't prevent an accidental injury, you'll at least be ready for it.

Resources

The American Red Cross.
Home Organizer for Medical Emergencies, from the American College of Emergency Physicians; (202) 728-0610.

FOOD

One day in 1992, six-year-old Lauren Beth Rudolph had a hamburger at a Carlsbad, CA, fast food restaurant. Four days later her kidneys failed because of an infection from the E.coli bacteria in the undercooked beef, and she died.

Have you ever had the twenty-four-hour flu? How about your child? Well, according to such experts as Charles P. Gerba, an environmental microbiologist and a professor at the University of Arizona, there is no such thing (since a true influenza infection lasts seven to ten days), which means what you *really* had was probably food poisoning.

You or your child could have picked up the bacteria that caused your illness, which probably included diarrhea and/or vomiting, anywhere you had something to eat, but Gerba says that at least 52 percent of the millions of annual cases of food poisoning are picked up at home-sweet-home.

And when the victims of food poisoning are children, the results are much more likely to be tragic. Their little bodies have a tough time fighting off a bacterial infection, so safe food handling is essential to anyone feeding a child.

To market, to market

When shopping, pick up perishable foods last and look carefully at anything you put into the cart.

- Fresh beef, poultry, and seafood should be properly refrigerated. The packaging should be undamaged. Fresh products should be carefully wrapped by store employees so that juices will not contaminate ready-to-eat foods in the cart.
- Eggs should be refrigerated, grade A or better, and undamaged.
- Dairy products should be refrigerated and undamaged.

Also remember to check the dates on any perishable items. Buy the freshest items possible, keeping in mind when you plan to use them. Take your food straight home from the store and refrigerate or freeze all perishable items immediately.

Perishable items should be stored in the coldest part of a refrigerator set at forty degrees Fahrenheit or colder—never in the door. Uncooked meat, fish, or poultry can be kept for one to two days in the refrigerator, or three to four months in the freezer. Cooked meat, fish, or poultry can be kept three to four days in the refrigerator, or two to three months in the freezer. Eggs and dairy products should never be stored or used past the date printed on the package.

The careful gourmet

Anything that comes in contact with your food has got to be clean—and cleaned again after it touches foods that might contain harmful bacteria. These include raw fish, chicken, beef, or eggs.

Wash your hands in warm soapy water before you start cooking, and disinfect work surfaces with an antibacterial soap, or by spritzing them lightly with a mixture of one teaspoon of bleach to a gallon of water and drying with paper towels—never a dish towel or sponge.

A 1995 study conducted by Dr. Gerba found that 20 percent of sponges and dishrags contained staphylococcus and/or salmonella, the two leading causes of food-borne illness in the United States, 54 percent contained bacteria that have the potential to cause illness in humans, and a huge proportion of sponges tested showed high levels of fecal coliform bacteria. Yuck! Run your sponges through the dishwasher or washer and dryer daily, and rinse well after each use to combat these nasty bacteria. Or microwave them for ninety seconds.

Home cooking

Thaw frozen beef, fish, or poultry in the refrigerator or in a microwave oven. Be aware, however, that you should never microwave these foods in their original polystyrene (Styrofoam) trays. The USDA warns that these containers, as well as cold-storage containers like margarine tubs and cottage-cheese cartons, are not heat stable at high temperatures. They can melt or warp from the food's heat and cause chemicals to migrate into the food.

While cooking, keep raw beef, fish, poultry, and eggs away from ready-to-eat foods that will not be cooked (such as salads). Thoroughly wash and disinfect any utensil, dish, or work surface that has come into contact with one of these raw foods before using them to prepare ready-to-eat foods. It is also important to wash your hands after handling raw foods, before preparing other foods, or before touching your child.

Cook beef at a temperature of 160 degrees Fahrenheit or higher until there is no pink left in the center, and all juices run clear. Poultry should be cooked until no pink remains in the center of the meat, and all juices run clear. Before serving, cut into the thickest part of meats to make sure they are done.

Fish is done when it looks solid, and flakes when tested with a fork. (Because of the danger of bacteria contamination, it is unsafe to serve raw fish at home.) Cook eggs until the white is firm and no longer opaque, and the yolk becomes firm.

Dinner is served

Make sure your child washes his hands before eating. It doesn't do any good to prepare food safely unless you are prepared to eat it safely, too.

Keep cooked foods hot until ready to serve, and refrigerate leftovers as soon as possible.

When reheating leftover beef, fish, or poultry, heat it to a temperature of at least 160 degrees, or until it is thoroughly hot and steamy. But again, be careful what containers you use in the microwave to avoid adding toxic chemicals to your meal.

Baby food

General rules of safe storage and preparation apply to foods for your baby, but some additional cautions are in order.

Honey and eggs should not be given to children younger than one, no matter how they are prepared. Eggs are sometimes contaminated with salmonella bacteria, and a salmonella infection could be deadly to an infant. While the salmonella threat can be eliminated by proper cooking, it isn't worth the risk. Honey is often contaminated with botulism bacteria, which poses no threat to older children or adults, but is poisonous to infants. Almost 95 percent of cases of botulism occur in children under six months old, according to *Your Child's Wellness Newsletter,* and the safest way to avoid it is by not feeding your baby honey. Remember that babies can also become infected by honey on the hands of siblings or caregivers.

When heating foods for your baby—especially when using the microwave—stir thoroughly before feeding to prevent hot spots, and test the food for temperature.

If your child is ready for table food, be sure that the food is cut into pieces small enough to prevent choking. Slice cylindrical foods such as hot dogs, bananas, and carrots up the middle before cutting them into pieces, and cut grapes in half.

Resources

E.coli 0157:H7: What You Need to Know If There Is an Outbreak in Your Community, from the United States Department of Agriculture, July 1995.

Dinner's Served, a video available through the San Diego County Department of Environmental Health; (619) 338-2195.

The Egg Handling & Care Guide, from the American Egg Board, 1460 Renaissance Dr., Park Ridge, IL 60068.

"What's the Catch," by Tamara Tuttle, *L.A. Parent* magazine, November 1995, pp. 32-34.

"Infants, Honey and the Threat of Botulism," *Your Child's Wellness Newsletter,* January/February 1996, p. 8.

USDA Meat and Poultry Hotline. (800) 535-4555.

GARAGE

If your garage is like mine, it serves as a catchall for just about anything you don't want in the house. It's a great place to keep stuff, but that makes it *not* a great place for kids.

I recommend doing everything you can to keep the kids out of the garage, but I know this is impossible. (For one thing, their bikes are probably housed there.) Even if you do not plan for your children to have access to the garage, the safest thing to do is assume that they will eventually find their way in there somehow, and childproof the place as if it were their regular playroom.

A big part of making the garage safe is taking a look at what you store there and how you store it.

Open sesame

If you have an automatic garage-door opener, make sure it is the kind that automatically reverses when it touches any object so your child doesn't get hurt if the door comes down while he's underneath.

Tool time

If the garage is where you hang your tool belt, make sure you hang it high. Kids like nothing better than to "fix" things, and while they may have your handyman (or woman) spirit, they probably haven't mastered your technique—or read the safety manual. Store your hand tools in a locked toolbox or secure them on a shelf well out of reach. (Keep in mind that kids will climb sawhorses and scale shelves.) Unplug power tools and disable them if you can (e.g., take the bit out of the power drill) and keep them out of reach as well.

If your power tools are the floor-model variety (a table saw, lathe, or drill press) you'll want to make sure they have a combination plug lock to make them impossible for your kids to turn on.

And, of course, it is important to remember to clean up after yourself and put all tools away when you are finished working. Even if you are interrupted and must leave a tool for only a minute, you should unplug it and move it out of reach.

Toxic offenders

The garage also seems like a good place to get dangerous cleaners and other products out of the way. Just make sure that they truly are out of reach. Hazards include:

gasoline
propane gas cylinders
kerosene
lighter fluid
cleaning products
oil-based paints
fertilizers
mineral spirits
furniture polish
floor polish

disinfectants
pesticides
weed killers
turpentine
toxic glues

Since many of these substances are not packaged in childproof containers, it is vital that they be stored out of reach, and under lock and key if at all possible. These products should be stored in their original containers, which are labeled with information about their contents, proper use, and disposal. If your child does come in contact with one of these substances, it is very important for emergency personnel to know exactly what they are dealing with.

Another hazardous feature of these products is their flammability. If a child takes one of these items near an ignition source—such as a furnace, water heater, stove, clothes dryer, electric appliance, or even a match—the fumes can ignite, causing an explosion or fire.

Cold storage

Old refrigerators or freezers, ice chests, and even washers and dryers are death traps to a child locked inside. The Consumer Product Safety Commission has reported the deaths of several children, most between the ages of four and seven, who climbed inside one of these appliances and couldn't get out again because the door couldn't be easily opened from the inside.

Most of these appliance doors feature tight-fitting gaskets and are insulated to keep in cold, heat, or water. Unfortunately, this insulation also keeps out air, and keeps a trapped child's screams from being heard.

It's best not to store refrigerators or freezers that are not in use, but if you cannot avoid it, remove the latch or the entire door to prevent children from being trapped. Another option is to stand the appliance with the door against a wall so that it cannot be opened. (If you do want to get rid of an old appliance, contact your city's municipal services department to find out about disposal and recycling programs.) Store ice chests either in the rafters, or put something heavy on top so your kids cannot get inside.

How things stack up

Many things that are not dangerous alone could be a hazard if they are in a precarious pile. Be careful of how you stack boxes and other objects, because when it all comes tumbling down, your child might be underneath. Put the larger, heavier items on the bottom, and never pile things too high.

Avoid storing items in plastic trash bags, or using plastic bags or drop cloths to protect things from dust or moisture. Children can become tangled in these and suffocate.

While you are working

You know how difficult it is to talk on the telephone or even read the newspaper when your kids are around. And the telephone won't saw off your thumb or sand through your skin. This means you probably don't want the little ones in attendance when you're using power tools. Kids are distracting, and that means one of you could get hurt.

If you are working with older children, make sure they are wearing the same protective gear you are (heavy shirt and pants, safety goggles, gloves, protective face shields for welding, etc.). And establish a no-talking rule whenever a tool is turned on. Any explaining that is necessary should be done before the tool is used.

Never allow children of any age to come into the garage with you if you are working with a dangerous chemical, such as a paint stripper. These can irritate the skin and eyes, cause headaches, drowsiness, nausea, or dizziness—especially to someone breathing the fumes. Since children use more oxygen per pound of body weight than adults, they will succumb more quickly to these fumes.

Garage talk

Above all, teach your children that anything found in the garage that does not belong to them is off-limits. Help them gain a healthy respect for tools and hazardous chemicals, and make it a rule that these things are never to be touched or used without your supervision.

And since no amount of childproofing is foolproof, don't let the kids use the garage as a place to play. No matter how good a job you have done at securing hazards, your creative child may discover one you haven't thought of.

Resources

"Keep Your Family and Home Safe from Flammable Vapors," from the National Safe Kids Campaign and the Gas Appliance Manufacturers Association. For child safety materials, call (800) GAMA-811.

"Hidden Hazards in Your Home," from the Alisa Ann Ruch Burn Foundation; (800) 242-BURN.

"CPSC Warns About Suffocation and Death of Children in Old Refrigerators," "CPSC Warns About Child Entrapment In Household Appliances and Picnic Coolers," "Safety Commission Warns About Eye Injuries from Welding," and "What You Should Know About Using Paint Strippers," from the Consumer Product Safety Commission; (800) 638-2772.

KeepSafe Catalog Company, a good source for combination plug locks and other safety devices; (800) 836-5544.

GUNS

There are an estimated 200 million guns in U.S. homes today. They are in half of all households, and kill thirty-eight thousand people a year. About five thousand of these are children (that's fourteen kids a day), and at least two hundred of these deaths are accidents. Despite the blur of statistics, it doesn't take colossal math skills to figure out that a house, minus a gun, is a safer house.

If you have a gun, keep in mind that nearly all accidental shootings of children happen in or around the home and involve guns that are kept loaded and accessible. Not surprising considering that half of all handguns are stored unlocked, 30 percent are kept loaded, and 13 percent are kept both unlocked and loaded.

Think your kids don't know where the guns are kept? Nearly 80 percent of children know where their parents keep their guns, says the National Safe Kids Campaign. Think your gun is safe because your child is too young to have the strength to fire it? Then you should know that at least 85 percent of three- to four-year-olds can fire a gun with a trigger pull strength of less than five pounds (the setting on 63 percent of firearms), according to a study of more than five hundred children by Sara Naureckas, M.D., of Children's Memorial Hospital in Chicago. In fact, children under six pull the trigger in about 8 percent of the 1,500 accidental shootings each year, according to a General Accounting Office study cited by Naureckas.

Get the lead out

If you're looking to get rid of a gun, your local law-enforcement agency should be more than happy to help.

Your first option is simply to call and see if they will send an officer to pick up the weapon. If they can't send someone, you should still call before bringing it to the station. Give a physical description of yourself and the gun or guns you will be bringing. Get specific instructions on how the gun must be transported (e.g., in the trunk of your car or the glove compartment), and write down the name of the person you speak to.

Many police departments have a "no questions asked" policy toward anyone turning in a gun and won't require you to give any information about yourself. However, some departments require you to leave your name and address. Guns turned in to the police are generally destroyed or resold, but the person turning in the weapon is not compensated.

You may be able to get something in exchange for the guns you turn in if you can find a buyback program in your community. These programs trade goods or services for unwanted guns, and the police are not allowed to ask any questions or record the names or license-plate numbers of people who participate. Your police department can usually give you information on when and where these events are scheduled.

A hard sell

If you can't bear to see your firearm destroyed—and see all that money go to waste—you can still get rid of your gun by selling it to an established gun dealer or at a gun show. In some states you must have a permit to sell a gun, and you may even be required to register changes in ownership. In any case, you should keep thorough records of gun transactions so you can prove that you no longer own the gun if it is later used in a crime. Of course, an old handgun may not be worth much money and you may have trouble finding someone to buy it.

Away from home

If you or your spouse and the weapons in question don't want to part company, you can at least store them away from home. Many shooting ranges rent secure lockers on a monthly or yearly basis. That way, the gun is safely stored where you can safely use it.

It probably isn't a good idea to store a gun in your safe deposit box, since most states have laws against carrying a weapon into a federally insured building (such as an FDIC bank).

In the house

There are plenty of products on the market—trigger locks, gun safes, lockboxes—that claim they can help you store your gun safely in your home. These options all cost money, however, and some are very expensive.

Some of these devices work on the principle that they are too complicated for a child to open. But given enough time, even the youngest child can find a way through virtually any safety barrier. My main problem with home-storage safety devices, however, is that they rely on the owner to remember to put them into effect. If the owner fails to properly close just one latch, one time, the gun is as dangerous as if it were left lying on the coffee table.

Not an option

One thing you should never do is attempt to disable a gun, or keep a gun that has been disabled in your home. Trying to fire a gun that has had the barrel bent, or filled with concrete or lead, can be dangerous because the gun will probably explode in the shooter's hand.

Resources _____

The HELP Handgun Disposal Handbook: A Prescription for Safety, published by the Handgun Epidemic Lowering Plan Network, a group of professionals dedicated to reducing the violence caused by handguns.

For a copy, send ten dollars to HELP Network, Children's Memorial Medical Center, 2300 Children's Plaza, Suite 88, Chicago, IL 60614, or call (312) 880-3826.

"Children's and Women's Ability to Fire Handguns," *The Archives of Pediatric Medicine*, volume 149, December, 1995, pp. 1318-1350.

"Unintentional Firearm Injury," from the National Safe Kids Campaign; (202) 884-4993.

Preventing Handgun Violence Against Kids: A Bibliography of Resources and References, from Prevent Handgun Violence Against Kids, a public education campaign of the California Wellness Foundation; (415) 331-3337.

Firearm Facts: Information on Gun Violence and Its Prevention, from the Children's Safety Network at the National Center for Education in Maternal and Child Health; (703) 524-7802.

HALLOWEEN

Ghoulies, ghosties, and loooong-leggedy beasties are far from the scariest things about Halloween. In fact, a witch brewing up a spell to cause accidents could hardly do better.

Start with the dark of night, then add crowds of excited children tangled in costumes, props, flashlights, and candy bags (for added punch, throw in a good-sized sugar rush and partially blind them with rubber masks). Throw in a few knives (for cutting pumpkins) and some burning jack-o'-lanterns. Then spill the whole mess right out into the street and watch the chaos begin.

Cutting your risk

Twice as many children under age eleven go to the emergency room with knife-related injuries during the three days before Halloween as during the rest of the year, according to a study by Failure Analysis Associates, an independent firm that investigates and analyzes accident data.

So how are kids who aren't even allowed to cut their own meat the rest of the year getting their hands on these blades? The annual carving of the sacrificial pumpkin, of course! To be sure you aren't sacrificing safety in the process, keep the kitchen knife in the drawer and use one of the widely available (and cheap) kids' pumpkin cutters. They are safer, and actually give kids better control. Another alternative is painting the pumpkin. If Mom or Dad is doing the carving and feels too grown up to use an orange piece of plastic with a goblin handle, make sure the kids are in bed before you start.

Safety in disguise

Another set of injury stats that takes a big jump right before All Hallows' Eve is scissor wounds to kids ages three to eleven, according to FaAA. These are kids who are either helping create their costume, or who find the sewing scissors their frantic mother left within reach while pondering how to turn three old sheets into Casper the Friendly Ghost and his sinister uncles.

These scenarios can be avoided by precutting pieces for arts, crafts, and costumes your child will put together, and by keeping careful tabs on the scissors whenever you are making costumes. Sitting down to work near a high shelf where you can stash the shears after every use is one option. Hanging them around your neck is another.

When making and choosing costumes for your child, see that everything fits properly. Serious injuries to children falling down stairs rise to 2,700 per day during Halloween, so make sure your children aren't encumbered by flowing capes or gowns that can get tangled around their legs, masks that keep them from seeing properly, or hats and wigs that slip down over their eyes.

And try not to load them down with too many props. Carrying a pitchfork, a flashlight, and a bag full of treats could trip up your little devil. These things could also get her tangled up in that brilliantly carved jack-o'-lantern burning on the neighbors' front porch. (If you buy your child's costume, make sure the label says it's flame resistant.)

Anything your child does carry—even pitchforks—should be made of soft, flexible material that won't do any damage to innocent bystanders. And make sure the kids' boots were made for walkin'. Mom's high heels are not the best accessory for this night on the town.

For best results, put the whole outfit (including props) together in advance and have your child go up and down your own front steps to make sure all is well.

Show it off

We costume our kids to be seen, and the most important people who should be able to see them are the drivers of cars out on Halloween night. If you've draped your child in seasonal black, add a few touches of reflective tape (available in hardware stores and bicycle shops) that will glow in drivers' headlights. Glow-in-the-dark masks and candy sacks make visible accessories.

Carrying a flashlight will help your little ghoul to see *and* be seen.

Walkin' the walk

Dracula probably never required a chaperon, but your miniature version does. Young children should have either an adult or an older child tag along. Older children should be taught that there's safety in numbers, and go in a group.

All trick-or-treaters should walk, not run, along the sidewalk from house to house. They should cross streets at the corner and never dart out from between parked cars—even if the house across the street is giving out Hershey bars. Kids should use the sidewalk to get up to the door, and never cross the lawn where they might trip over sprinkler heads or other obstacles. And once they've made it to the door, they should remember never to go inside a house or apartment without their parents' permission.

After the ball

Very few injuries involve candy that has been tampered with, but children should still be told not to eat treats that have not been inspected by Mom or Dad.

Thoroughly inspect each piece of candy, throwing out anything that is unwrapped. If you have a child under age three, you might also want to take out small, hard candies, bubble gum, and anything else that presents a choking hazard. You can always substitute some safe treats of your own if your tot feels shortchanged. If you have more than one child, big brother or sister can take the little one's hard candy and gum in trade for some safer treats.

Resources

"Keeping Little Spirits Safe on Halloween" and "The Costume Safety Rap," from the National Safety Council.
"Halloween Safety Guidelines," from Failure Analysis Associates Inc.
"Halloween Safety," from the U.S. Consumer Product Safety Commission.

HIGH CHAIRS

When it comes to feeding toddlers, some people worry about nutrition, while others dread the inevitable meeting of strained peas and new dining-room carpet. But thousands of babies are treated in emergency rooms every year for injuries associated with high chairs—so it isn't falling food that should be your main concern.

Taking the high road

Most of the injuries, in fact, are caused by falling chairs and/or falling children, so make sure your child's high chair has a wide base for stability.

Also keep in mind that a high chair is not a restraining device where you can leave your child unsupervised. Use the chair only when you are close at hand. Children who are left by themselves in a high chair will inevitably get bored and try to make an escape. This might involve standing up in the high chair, pushing off with their hands and feet from a nearby wall or table, or rocking the chair back and forth. It is also certain to result in a fall and a boo-boo the child wasn't bargaining for.

To help keep your little climber in check, choose a chair with a sturdy waist strap and a strap that runs between the legs. (Of course, the straps do no good unless you use them every time you bring child and chair together.) The crotch strap is essential, because it prevents the child from wriggling out under the tray and being strangled by the tray or the waist strap—which is how most high-chair-related deaths occur.

It is also a good idea to position the chair out of reach of tables, walls, or anything else the child might use to tip the chair over. Never let your child climb into or out of a high chair without your help, and don't let older children climb or hang on to the chair. They might tip it over.

If your chair is metal, caps or plugs at the ends of the tubing should be firmly attached so they can't pull off and choke a child. If yours is a folding chair, make sure it has a locking device to keep it from collapsing during the main course.

If you're hooked

Hook-on chairs are a convenient option for families on the go, or those who want to give junior a place at the table. These chairs fit onto the table itself, which then doubles as a feeding tray. But take care when choosing and using one, or your child may end up under the table rather than at it.

All hook-on chairs should have a safety strap to keep the child in place and a clamp that locks onto the table and helps keep the chair in place. Caps on metal tubing should be secure to avoid choking hazards. And when choosing your child's place, take a look under the table to make sure there is nothing she can use to hurl herself backward with her feet.

Use a hook-on seat only on tables sturdy enough not to break or tip over under their weight, and never use them on pedestal or glass-topped tables. Take a look *on* the table to see that the crystal goblets and the steak knives are out of reach.

Resources

Equipment Safety Checklist and *The Safe Nursery Buyer's Guide,* from the U.S. Consumer Product Safety Commission; (800) 638-2772.

"Safe and Sound for Baby," from the Juvenile Product Manufacturers Association, 2 Greentree Centre, Box 955, Marlton, NJ 08053.

INDOOR AIR

Whether the view from your kitchen window includes gray urban haze or a breezy country meadow, the air out there isn't nearly as important as the air on the other side of the glass. Even in the most congested cities, the air indoors can be ten to one hundred times more polluted than the great outdoors, according to the National Air Duct Cleaners Association.

This could mean health problems from runny nose, itchy eyes, and scratchy throat to headaches, fatigue, and respiratory infections—maybe even asthma. This makes cleaning up your indoor air act important for everyone in your family.

Yucky stuff that is probably in your air

- House dust, which contains delightful ingredients like cloth fibers, pollen, mold spores, insect fragments, rubber, fireplace soot, shed scales of human skin, and house dust mites, is one of the major contributors to indoor air pollution. And even if you aren't allergic or asthmatic, do you really want your family breathing this stuff?
- Organic gases from household products like paint and paint strippers, aerosol sprays, hobby supplies, and ironically, cleaners, disinfectants, and air fresheners can all find their way into your indoor air, where they do more harm than good.

Yucky stuff that *might* be in your air

- Tobacco smoke sends four million children a year to the doctor, and causes 307,000 cases of asthma, 354,000 ear infections, 5,200 operations to insert ear tubes, and 14,000 operations to remove tonsils every year, according to a study by Joseph DiFranza reported in the April 1996 issue of *Pediatrics*. This should be reason enough to keep this indoor air pollutant outdoors.
- Radon is a colorless, odorless natural pollutant that is worth testing for. (See "Radon.")
- Carbon monoxide and nitrogen dioxide can be pumped into your home by improperly functioning fireplaces or appliances. (See Carbon Monoxide.")

- Formaldehyde finds its way into your home via pressed-wood products like paneling, foam insulation, and glues (such as carpet glue).
- Pesticides are sometimes used to kill household pests, and aren't good for humans, either. Even those used in the yard can be tracked into the house.
- Asbestos might be in your home in the form of insulation materials. (See "Asbestos.")
- Lead can work its way into the home via dust and dirt, automobile exhaust, or old paint. (See "Lead.")
- Fiberglass might be contained in your home's insulation, or your furnace and air-conditioner filters.

Why bad air hurts kids more

While no one wants to breathe any of the aforementioned substances, they are extra harmful to children, who breathe more air per pound of body weight than do adults. Kids also spend more time near the floor, stirring up the dust containing these pollutants. All this pollution is quite a challenge for their still-developing immune systems, so the result is often respiratory infections, or even asthma.

What you can do about it

Start your crusade for cleaner air in the bedroom, where your kids spend at least 40 percent of their time.

- Encase mattresses and pillows in zippered, dustproof covers, and choose pillows and comforters made with synthetic fibers.
- Wash bedding in hot water (warm water won't kill dust mites) weekly. Shake out bedspreads outdoors every few days if possible.
- Eliminate as much dust-catching clutter as possible.

- If your child has asthma or allergies, put stuffed animals in the freezer for twenty-four hours once a week to kill dust mites, then wash them to remove dead mites and their droppings. Researchers at Southampton University in England reported in 1995 that this was the most effective eradication method.
- Keep pets out of the bedroom.
- Keep windows closed at night, and use the air conditioning to help filter the air.

There are other things you can do to keep the air clearer throughout the house:

- Remove carpets and drapes, if possible. They hold dust mites and mold, and mildew if they get wet. If this isn't possible, you can apply a nontoxic tannic-acid solution to kill mites, and vacuum frequently with doors and windows open to help combat dust. Ideally, you should use a vacuum with a HEPA air filter.
- Dust with a damp cloth so you don't send particles back into the air.
- Air out your house as frequently as possible.
- Make sure stoves, portable heaters, and fireplaces are in good condition and vented properly. Keep air-conditioning and heating ducts clean.
- If you smoke, don't do it indoors, or near open doors or windows.
- Choose the least toxic versions of household cleaners (for instance, Bon Ami cleanser over Ajax, which contains chlorine bleach), and keep your house clean and well ventilated to eliminate the need for air fresheners.
- Buy only exterior-grade pressed-wood paneling and furniture, which emits less formaldehyde. Air the house as much as possible after bringing these products into your home.
- Minimize use of pesticides, or try an organic version.
- Consider having the family take off their shoes before coming into the house so you won't track in so much dust and dirt.

- Seek professional help if you suspect you have a lead, asbestos, fiberglass, or radon problem.
- Try using a dehumidifier to keep the humidity level below 50 percent if you are having difficulty with mold and mildew.
- If you think all this just isn't enough, you might want to try a HEPA-type air filter to get your domestic atmosphere squeaky clean.

Resources

"Cleaning House," by Scott Trimingham, *L.A. Parent* magazine, February 1996, p. 60.

The Indoor Air Project Guide to Healthy Indoor Air; (310) 378-0260.

"Does Your Home Suffer from Indoor Air Pollution?", from the National Air Duct Cleaners Association; 1518 K. St. N.W., Suite 503, Washington, D.C., 20005.

"Breathing Space: What You Can Do to Stop the Rise of Asthma," by Mindy Pennybacker, *The Green Guide,* issue 21, March 1, 1996.

INFANT CARRIER SEATS

Infant seats make your baby conveniently portable, allowing you to take her from place to place and keep her nearby during those rare moments when you aren't feeding her, changing her, or rocking her to sleep. They are also a nice way to prop her up for a look at the world she was born into.

The downside of these devices is that people use them to stash babies in places where babies really shouldn't be—like on the kitchen counter. The majority of infant-seat injuries aren't caused by the seat itself, but by where the seat is placed. Here are a few guidelines for using your seat safely:

- Choose a seat with a wide, sturdy base for stability.
- Place your seat only on the floor or on firm, sturdy surfaces where it won't tip over. Don't use the carrier on glass-topped tables, countertops, beds, or other upholstered furniture. When your baby's seat is on an elevated surface, make sure it isn't too close to the edge.
- Stay within arm's reach of your baby whenever his seat is on an elevated surface, and never leave baby unattended in the seat— even for a minute.
- Make sure your baby is a safe distance from anything she could use to push off with her feet. Also clear the area of any hazardous object that shouldn't be within baby's reach (i.e., small objects he could choke on, scissors, medications).
- If the seat doesn't have nonskid feet, cover the feet with the same kind of nonskid safety strips you would use in the bottom of a bathtub.
- If your seat has some kind of bracket or supporting device on the back that keeps it upright, make sure it is secured every time you put your baby in.
- Your carrier should have both a waist and crotch strap with an easy-to-use buckle, and you should fasten them every time you use the seat.
- Unless your carrier/seat is designed to double as a car seat, do not use it in the car.

Resources

The Safe Nursery Buyer's Guide and "Nursery Equipment Safety Checklist," from the U.S. Consumer Product Safety Commission; (800) 638-2772.

"Safe and Sound for Baby," from the Juvenile Products Manufacturers Association, 2 Greentree Centre, Box 955, Marlton, NJ 08053.

KITCHEN

Much of the babyproofing advice I have read revolves around using baby gates and locks to keep your children out of the kitchen, but I don't buy it (or them). I believe the benefits of learning about and helping prepare healthy food far outweigh the hazards found in this room—especially if you take the proper precautions.

Drawers and cupboards

To avoid having your child sliced, diced, grated, and julienned, it's prudent to keep certain things out of reach. The list of kitchen gadgets with small parts (a choking hazard) or sharp edges is too long to print here. And your stack of dinnerware no doubt includes some breakables. You know what they are. The problem is where to keep them.

Cabinet and drawer latches may be the first thing that comes to mind, but I don't care for this option because I've seen how fast a kid with a will can conquer any obstacle when it means reaching something forbidden. If your two-year-old has mastered the TV remote well enough to locate Barney, don't you think he can puzzle out a simple cabinet latch? You, on the other hand, might have some trouble—especially with your big, fat adult fingers.

Instead, I recommend storing sharp stuff and glass stuff high. If you have to, put the sharp knives and gadgets in a box on an upper shelf. It's worth the inconvenience, since about sixteen thousand children under age five were hurt playing with knives in a single year (1993), according to the CPSC. You should also move plastic bags and plastic wrap, which suffocate about fifteen kids a year, away from child level.

Save the lower shelves and drawers for the pots and pans and Tupperware. In fact, giving your children the run of one or two drawers or cabinets filled with harmless items might help keep them occupied so they're not underfoot when you're chopping, stirring, or pouring.

If your kitchen is so tight on space that you are forced to store breakables or sharp items in a cabinet or drawer your child can reach, buy and install some good-quality safety latches, and keep a close eye on your child to make sure she hasn't learned to use them. This precaution should be combined with a firm "no" every time you see your child at the cabinet in question. Redirect him to a cabinet where you have stored items you don't mind him playing with.

While you're busy moving and locking up the dangerous items, don't forget the trash. If you can't move the can out of reach, buy a can with a lid that latches closed. These things won't keep your child out completely, but will probably slow her down. As an extra precaution, plastic bags should be knotted before they are thrown away, and anything particularly dangerous (empty bottles of household cleaner, broken glass, sharp can lids) should be carried to the trash can outdoors.

The cleaner clean-out

Keep cleaning products out of reach—which means *not* under the kitchen sink. A high shelf in a locked cabinet is the best place for cleaners, and since you don't want to store these products next to dishes or food, that probably means moving them to another room. If you can't find a safe place (that's convenient, so you'll actually *put* the cleaners there), a latch on the undersink cabinet might be your only option. Just remember to keep all hazardous cleaning products there at all times, and make sure the latch is secure.

On a related topic, have you recently completed an entire house-cleaning task without being interrupted? These interruptions might cause you to leave a box or bottle of something nasty temporarily unprotected, so it's best to choose the least toxic items possible.

The Washington Toxics Coalition recommends label reading as

the best place to start. While label warnings won't tell you every-thing, it isn't hard to learn what to look for.

"Poison," "harmful if swallowed," "flammable," "corrosive," and "irritant" should all tip you off that this stuff isn't good for kids. And the word "danger" means exactly that—a taste to a teaspoon of one of these products could be fatal. "Warning" and "caution" often mean the same thing. These are not products you want to have sitting around your house. If you must buy something with this type of warning on the label, buy as little as possible and take extra care where you keep it.

Washington Toxics also warns against using products containing the following ingredients:

- Chlorinated compounds (anything with the prefix "chlor" in the ingredient list).
- Aerosols, which put chemicals into the air where they can be inhaled.
- Lye or sodium hydroxide, which can cause severe burns.
- Phenols, which are highly toxic chemicals and serious water pollutants.
- Petroleum distillates, which are flammable and very dangerous if swallowed.

Even if they appear pretty safe, keep all cleaning products away from children. Automatic-dishwasher detergent, which most peo-ple think of as just another form of soap, is as caustic as drain cleaner if swallowed.

You could also choose to do your cleaning with nontoxic recipes made from household items. Vinegar and water, for in-stance, works well as a floor cleaner. Baking soda will help clear your clogged drain, and is good for scrubbing countertops. If you decide to go this route, call the Washington Toxics Coalition at (206) 632-1545 and ask for their Safe Cleaning Kit recipes. They have a concoction for almost every cleaning job.

Countertop tips

Keep appliances such as coffeemakers, blenders, and toasters at the back of the counter, and keep their cords wound up so that children can't use them to pull the appliance off the counter and onto their little heads. Keep these appliances unplugged when you're not using them, both as a fire safety measure and to make sure your child doesn't accidentally turn one on.

And be aware of where you're setting things while you are cooking. If you are chopping vegetables, make sure you don't put the knife down near the edge of the counter. If you are using a glass mixing bowl, don't leave it where your child could knock it over. If you take a hot pot or pan off the stove, put it somewhere your child can't reach.

They can't stand the heat

Since more than seven thousand children are burned by stoves each year, there are plenty of stove-knob covers and other gadgets designed to limit kids' access to this appliance. These are great until your child figures a way around them. And since every house your child visits is not likely to have them, I think you'll be safest simply teaching your kids that the stove is hot.

I recommend not allowing infants and toddlers to touch any part of the stove, and reinforcing this by saying, "No. Hot!" whenever they do. It doesn't matter that they don't know what the word "hot" means. If you are consistent, the lesson will stick. Let older children watch what the stove does to food, and they'll get the idea.

But unfortunately, the stove isn't the only thing in the kitchen that gets hot. More than twenty thousand children are scalded by hot liquids or foods every year, according to the National Safe Kids Campaign. Not surprising considering the temperatures foods reach during cooking—five hundred degrees for deep frying, four hundred degrees for baking, three hundred degrees for frying, and two hundred for a Crock-Pot—which can cause second- and third-degree burns in less than a second.

Keep pot handles on the stove turned in when cooking so children cannot reach them, and pay attention to where you are putting dishes that contain hot food. If children are waiting at the table while you bring out platters of hot food, make sure they are supervised so they don't burn themselves.

Micro-wave—macro-burns

The microwave oven may seem pretty child safe—there are no flames or exposed heating elements, no hot pans, no boiling kettles. But about 2,300 children a year are severely burned by food or infant formula that has been microwaved, according to the National Safe Kids Campaign. Kids can be burned by hot spots in food that appears cool enough to eat, steam escaping when a microwaved container of food is opened, or the filling in pies, tarts, or doughnuts, which can reach temperatures of six hundred degrees or higher.

To prevent these burns:

- Heat food and infant formula only in microwave-safe bottles or containers.
- Use an oven mitt when removing food from the microwave. Grabbing a hot dish with your bare hands could cause you to spill it on your child.
- Open just-microwaved containers carefully. Escaping steam can cause a painful burn.
- Shake the bottle or stir the food, then check the temperature before feeding your child.
- Supervise young children using the microwave, and teach older children to do it safely. Never let children take food out of a microwave oven on a shelf too high for them to reach comfortably. Hot food could spill on their hands and face.

Someone's in the kitchen with Mama (or Dad)

There are several proven (by me) methods for keeping kitchen-loving kids out of harm's way—and yours.

- Babies are often easiest to keep busy in their high chair. This keeps them up at your level where they can see what's going on. Handing them a plastic dish or wooden spoon and keeping up a running conversation about what you are doing is often enough to hold their interest. Just make sure you place the high chair far away from the stove, and out of reach of countertops.
- Toddlers are often appeased by the amazing Tupperware drawer distraction. Gather up all the extra pots, pans, Tupperware, and other harmless gadgets you don't use very often, and load them into an easy-to-reach drawer or cabinet. This is your child's special "cooking" place. Save this spot for times when the two of you can "cook" together, and add items occasionally to keep it interesting.

Cooking with kids

Of course your best opportunity to keep kids busy in the kitchen is by cooking with them.

Kids will probably be willing to help before they are able to handle many kitchen jobs, according to Molly Katzen, noted author of *Pretend Soup and Other Real Recipes* and many other cookbooks. "The interest will usually precede fine motor coordination," she says, adding that this doesn't mean kids can't "cook."

"You can have them sit on the floor with a bowl of clean water and a brush and wash vegetables," Katzen suggests, adding they can wipe the table or watch you stir something and tell you when it looks ready. "I would tell my daughter [when she was two and a half], 'This cake has raisins in it. Could you count the raisins for me?' Of course, I didn't really need the raisins counted, but I made it sound really important, and it would take her a long time." These types of peripheral jobs, explains Katzen, keep kids safely and happily engaged, and free your hands to do the serious work.

The day will come when your child is actually able to help with real cooking projects, but it will probably come before he is tall enough to reach the counter. Don't put kids up on a high stool to help them reach, warns Katzen. Instead bring the cooking down to their level by setting up a workstation on a low table, or even at the kitchen table where they have a booster seat. This may also mean purchasing a good-quality electric skillet. "Kids as young as three can cook with heat, but you should not have them up at the stove," Katzen explains.

One important thing to teach children is to have a firm grip on the spoon or spatula when they are stirring hot food. Dropping the spoon could splatter hot stuff all over them.

And as with all things, supervision is required—especially if your child is younger than eight or ten. This means you are there to help with things kids can't do for themselves, and remind them of safety rules:

- Kids should wait to taste hot foods until they get an okay from an adult.
- No one under age eight or ten takes things in or out of the oven, a food processor, a blender, etc.
- Never leave a child under eight alone in the kitchen with a plugged-in appliance.
- Kids under eight or ten should only cut with a plastic serrated picnic knife or a dinner knife. Any food that cannot be cut with one of these knives should be cut by an adult.
- No one under age five should grate. If your child is old enough, make sure he is grating a piece of food big enough to allow him a firm, safe grip. "It's when you drop the food that you scrape your knuckles," says Katzen.

While it's important for kids to learn the rules, it's also important for them to learn the reasons behind them. "Another big part of being safe in the kitchen is not just saying no, it's telling them why and showing them why," says Katzen. You should explain to kids that there is a sharp blade in the food processor that could hurt them, that the stove is hot, that the cheese grater is sharp, etc..

It's easier to follow safe cooking practices if you're not in a hurry. This means you don't want to start a big cooking project with your child when you have a hungry family waiting. "I would not have the goal of cooking with a child be dinner," suggests Katzen. "I think cooking with kids should be recreational."

Once your child is over age eight or ten, they can do a bit more in the kitchen. But Katzen says make sure you ask the child what they are comfortable with. "Always err on the side of being overly cautious. And when your kids get older and it's bothering them, they'll let you know."

Resources

Pretend Soup and Other Real Recipes, by Molly Katzen and Ann Henderson, (Tricycle Press, 1994). This is a great recipe book full of fun projects for kids, that always keeps safety in mind. Includes a section of safe cooking tips.

"Dangers in the Kitchen," *The New York Times,* January 26, 1995.

"Burn Savers Prevent Scalds," from the Alisa Ann Ruch Burn Foundation; (800) 242-BURN.

"Recipe for Safer Cooking," from the American Association of Home Appliance Manufacturers, 20 North Wacker Dr., Suite 1500, Chicago, IL 60606.

"Scald Burn Injury," from the National Safe Kids Campaign; (202) 884-4993.

"Kitchen Fire Safety," from the National Fire Protection Association, Batterymarch Park, Quincy, MA 02269-9101.

"Baby Safety Shower," and "Poison Lookout Checklist," from the U.S. Consumer Product Safety Commission.

"Safer Cleaning Products," by Jennie Goldberg, "A Safer Home: Reducing Your Use of Hazardous Household Products," by Carl Woestwin, and *Buy Smart, Buy Safe: A Consumer Guide to Less-Toxic Products,* by Phillip Dickey, from the Washington Toxics Coalition; (206) 632-1545.

LEAD

You probably know something about the dangers of lead, but don't think you're safe just because you don't live in an old house and have never caught your child eating paint chips. The U.S. Centers for Disease Control and Prevention estimates that one out of every eleven children in the United States has dangerous levels of lead in his body—even if he looks and acts healthy. People can be exposed in a number of ways:

• Paint containing lead
• Imported vinyl mini-blinds
• Contaminated soil in the yard
• Contaminated housedust
• Contaminated drinking or cooking water
• Lead crystal or lead-glazed porcelain and pottery
• Hobbies that use lead, such as pottery or stained-glass making
• Industry that pollutes the air with lead
• Lead contamination anywhere your child regularly spends time

You won't see the effects of lead poisoning right away, but they can be devastating. Lead can damage the brain and nervous system, cause behavior and learning problems, stunt your child's growth, and impair your child's hearing. Exposure can also cause headaches, high blood pressure, digestive problems, nerve disorders, and joint and muscle pain in children and adults. Pregnant women are especially at risk, and lead can even cause reproductive problems in both men and women.

Testing their "metal"

Children are at a much greater risk of being exposed to lead than adults, because they just plain put their hands in their mouths more, allowing more lead to enter their bodies. And because these bodies are still developing and absorb lead more easily, there is greater chance of long-term damage.

If you suspect your child has been exposed to high levels of lead over a period of time, talk to your pediatrician about having her blood tested. This is the only way to be certain of your child's lead level. Blood should be drawn from the vein (unpleasant though this may be), because the traditional finger prick can give false readings. These tests are often available at little or no charge through your local health department.

If your child has a high level of lead, treatment may range from changes in diet or a course of medication to a hospital stay.

Getting the lead out

Whether or not your child's blood lead level is high, it doesn't hurt to make sure your home is lead-free. Continued exposure to lead could create health problems for the whole family in the future—even if you're all just fine right now.

You should consider testing your home for lead, or having a professional do so, if:

• Your house was built before 1978, when the government severely reduced the lead levels allowed in paint.
• You have vinyl mini-blinds. (New lead-free mini-blinds were put

on the market in late 1996, and the lead in imported blinds was restricted, but existing blinds were not pulled off the market.)

- The water pipes in your home contain lead or lead solder (which is likely, since lead solder wasn't banned by the government until 1988).
- You live in or near a heavily industrial area.
- You regularly use old or imported dishes or pottery.

A professional lead-hazard assessment, which involves X-raying painted surfaces and testing samples of dirt and dust inside the home and out, can usually be had for $200 to $400, and is worth the expense if you have children under age six. Testing kits are also available in all shapes and sizes to help you detect lead in paint. *Consumer Reports* rated several in its July 1995 issue, and found most simple and fairly accurate. You can also contact the National Lead Information Center Clearinghouse at (800) 424-LEAD for information on professional testing.

Consumer Reports doesn't recommend using a home test kit to check your water for lead. Those they reviewed were found to be inaccurate, and you can obtain a reliable test for around twenty dollars from a lab. They mention Clean Water Lead Test Inc., (704) 251-6800; Environmental Law Foundation, (510) 208-4555; and SAVE, (718) 626-3936.

Lead in paint

If you find that some of the paint in your home contains high levels of lead, and the paint is in good condition, it may be best just to leave it alone. It's when the paint is crumbling or disturbed by removal or remodeling that lead dust gets into the air—and into your child's body. However, you may still want to cover it with wallpaper, paneling, or new paint to keep dust from forming in the future.

Lead paint that is deteriorating needs immediate attention—especially if it is in high-traffic areas like doors or windowsills.

If the job is small (such as a windowsill), you may be able to handle it yourself if you take the right precautions. Dust control is the key, and *Consumer Reports* suggests the following precautions:

- Seal off the work area by covering the floors, furniture, doors, and windows with heavy plastic.
- Rent or buy a HEPA respirator and wear plastic booties over your shoes.
- Wet the work surface with a spray bottle if you must scrape or sand peeling paint, and use a wet/dry abrasive. If the surface is too far gone, remove the paint using a chemical stripper.
- When the work is done, roll up any chips and debris inside the plastic cloths, wrap the entire bundle in plastic, and throw it away. Then use a HEPA vacuum if possible, wash the room, and vacuum again before painting. And don't forget to put your clothes straight into the wash.

Jobs where the paint is in bad condition all over usually require a professional. Look for a contractor who will use all the techniques just described, and has completed a course at an EPA lead-abatement training center. But consider full-scale lead removal only as a last resort. It can cost thousands of dollars.

Lead in water (see "Water")

If your water tests positive for lead, there are three reasonable long-term solutions.

1. Purchase a reverse-osmosis filter.
2. Buy a distiller to filter the water.
3. Install (and yes, you can do this yourself) a filter either under the sink or on the countertop to remove the lead. These cost around $100.

Using lead-free water for cooking is essential, since foods stewed or boiled in water with lead absorb the metal in concentrated amounts.

If you're overexposed

Whether or not you have discovered a major lead hazard in your home, there are plenty of good habits you can get into that will reduce your family's exposure to lead:

- Rehang sticky doors and wax hard-to-move window sashes to prevent dust from forming.
- Clean floors, windowsills and frames, and other high-traffic surfaces weekly with a solution of powdered automatic dishwasher detergent that contains phosphates and warm water. Rinse your rag, mop, or sponge in a separate bucket of clear water to avoid contaminating the cleaning solution, and change the rinse water frequently. Most multipurpose cleaners will not remove lead.
- Avoid dry sweeping, dusting, and vacuuming (unless your vacuum has a HEPA filter). This just puts more dust in the air where your kids can breathe it.
- Wash toys and stuffed animals regularly.
- Take your shoes off before entering your home so you don't track in lead-contaminated soil.
- Wash your children's hands a lot—especially before they eat or go to bed.
- Feed your kids foods that are low in fat and high in iron and calcium so they will absorb less lead.

Resources _____

"Lead in Paint: Controlling the Hazard" and "Lead in Water: Pipe Nightmares?", from *Consumer Reports*, July 1995, pp. 460-463. For reprints of this report, write: CU/Reprints, 101 Truman Ave., Yonkers, NY 10703-1057.

Protect Your Family From Lead in Your Home and The Inside Story: A Guide to Indoor Air Quality, from the U.S. Environmental Protection Agency. For information, call the National Lead Information Center at (800) LEAD-FYI, or (800) 424-LEAD. Or call the EPA's Safe Drinking Water Hotline at (800) 426-4791.

"CPSC Find Lead Poisoning Hazard for Young Children in Imported Vinyl Miniblinds" and "What You Should Know About Lead Based Paint in Your Home: Safety Alert," from the U.S. Consumer Product Safety Commission; (800) 638-2772.

MEDICINES

A well-stocked supply of medicines to treat your family's ills is essential, but it is equally essential to make sure these products that were meant to heal do not end up causing harm. About 1.2 million children under age six are poisoned by medications every year, according to Children's Hospital of Pittsburgh and the Cincinnati Drug and Poison Information Center.

These types of accidents are almost always preventable.

How to store it

Your first step is to make sure your child can't get into medications she shouldn't, and this means storing them properly. First, keep medicines in their original containers. The original packaging lists the proper dosing information, the number of pills or amount of liquid the package contains, drug interaction warnings, and the exact ingredients of the medication—information that is vital if you suspect your child has swallowed something he shouldn't.

Your next task is to make sure all medicines are either out of reach, or better yet, locked up. This may mean the medicine cabinet is not the best place for them, since children can often climb from the toilet to the sink and get easy access. I learned from my mom that a shoe box in the top of the linen closet was a better alternative.

One place you should definitely not be storing medication is your purse. Children have a fascination with purses and briefcases, and will explore their contents anytime they get a chance. You should also break the habit of keeping medicines on your dresser or nightstand, or on kitchen counters or cupboards. These places may make taking your medicine convenient for you, but they will also make getting into it convenient for your child.

Even vitamins must be kept out of reach. Many vitamins—especially prenatal vitamins taken by pregnant women—contain levels of iron that could be fatal to a child. In fact, iron is the leading cause of fatal ingestion poisonings in children under three, according to the Nonprescription Drug Manufacturers' Association. This means you have to be careful with any adult or children's supplement containing iron.

No matter how careful you are, you should still get medications in child-resistant containers whenever possible, just in case. But keep in mind that child-resistant does not mean child-impossible-to-open. Given enough time, kids can overcome any obstacle.

The medicine checkup

Give your medicine supply a regular checkup, and throw out anything that is past its expiration date, has changed color, or is giving off an odor it shouldn't. You should also get rid of any prescriptions you no longer need and any medication you can't identify. While you're at it, take notice of what medications you have on hand, and about how much is left in each bottle. This information could prove valuable in an emergency.

Being prepared

One thing you should definitely store with your medications is syrup of ipecac, a liquid that induces vomiting and could save your child's life in the event of a poisoning. You should never use ipecac without the advice of a poison control specialist, because vomiting could sometimes make things worse, but you should keep enough on hand to dose each of your children simultaneously if you needed to.

Another thing that's good to have on hand is medical-grade charcoal. These capsules can help soak up the poison in a child's stomach, and keep it from reaching the rest of the body. But again, they should be used only on the advice of a doctor or poison specialist.

Medical school

It also helps to teach your children a few things about why we have medications and how they can be dangerous. Children should know that they should only take medicine given by an adult, and that they should never take someone else's medicine. You should also point out that all forms of medication can be dangerous, including pills, liquids, ointments, and sprays.

Giving prescription medications

Sometimes, ironically, a child is harmed by prescription medication given by a loving parent or caregiver. The Department of Health and Human Services estimates that nearly half of children taking prescription medication are taking it incorrectly. Almost 5 percent of children admitted to the hospital are there because of misuse of medicine, and about half of those cases are serious or fatal.

There are several things parents do when giving medication that could harm their children:

- *Stopping the medication too soon.* This is especially true in the case of antibiotics. Just because a child feels better doesn't mean the bug that caused the illness is completely vanquished. If you don't give the full course of medication, your child could become reinfected. What's worse, the organism that was left alive is now stronger, and requires a stronger medication.
- *Not giving medicine at the right time.* Some medications must stay at certain levels in the bloodstream in order to work. If a dose is missed, the amount in the blood decreases and the medication can't work properly. This may mean waking a sleeping child, but having her get well faster will be worth it.
- *Missing doses because your child refuses to take the medicine.* Sometimes these things don't taste good, but drugs don't work if your child won't take them. If you know there's a medication your child particularly dislikes, ask your doctor if there is an alternative you can use. Or maybe you can try one of the new antibiotics that must be given only once or twice a day, so there are fewer battles.

  If not, don't try to hide the medication in food or drinks; it will only make your child distrust you and refuse to eat. Just be firm, hog-tie them if you have to, and get that medication where it belongs. Afterward, you can offer a treat to help the bad taste go away.
- *Giving too much or too little medication.* Don't give a little extra medication for good measure. The dosage your doctor prescribed was carefully calculated based on your child's weight. Taking more than this amount is considered an overdose.

You should also make sure you aren't giving too little. Shake bottles of liquid medication thoroughly so the active ingredient makes it onto the spoon, and always use a measuring spoon or medicine cup to measure medication. The teaspoon you use to stir your coffee isn't accurate.

To avoid mistakes with prescription medications, it is important to have all possible information about the prescription. Find out from the doctor writing the prescription the brand name and generic name of the medication he is ordering, and what it is supposed to do. That way you can check to make sure the pharmacy has filled the prescription correctly.

Your pharmacist should be able to tell you the proper dose of the medication for your child (compare this with what is written on the label and ask about any discrepancies), when and for how long to take it, what foods or beverages to avoid while taking the medication, and any possible side effects. She may also be able to provide written information for you to take home.

Giving over-the-counter medicines

Even over-the-counter medications can be dangerous if misused. Acetaminophen, the active ingredient in nonaspirin pain relievers such as Tylenol, is given to children for everything from fever to teething pain to the flu, but an overdose of this drug can lead to serious liver problems, and even death.

And parents are the ones who give the overdose 80 percent of the time, according to a report in the June 1995 issue of *Medical Tribune*. Sometimes parents don't read the label, so they think they are giving 80mg (the dose in a chewable tablet) when they are really giving 160mg (the dose in a junior caplet). Or they don't realize that the child's suspension liquid is a lot more potent than the infant suspension drop formula.

Another way parents unknowingly overdose their children is by giving them a pain reliever with acetaminophen along with a cold medication that also contains acetaminophen.

To avoid this and other problems with over-the-counter medications:

• *Know your child's current weight* so you can determine the proper dosage.

- *Read and follow the instructions on the label carefully* every time you give your child a medication. This will help you give the correct dosage (which will change as your child grows), and remind you of any warnings concerning the medicine.
- *Always check the expiration date* to make sure the medicine has not spoiled.
- *Use a real measuring device* such as a medicine spoon or measuring spoon to measure medication correctly.
- *Call your doctor* before giving your child two medications at the same time, if you are unsure of the proper dose, or if the medication is not working.
- *Never give your child medication that is meant for adults.*

No matter what form of medication you are using, keep an accurate record of the time and amount of each dose you have administered. Everyone giving the child medicine should record the information in the same place. And always check with your spouse or other caregivers in the home before giving medication, to avoid double dosing.

It is also important that you avoid describing medicine as "candy" in order to bribe your child into taking it. If she later finds the medication unguarded, she may remember what you said and decide to take some on her own.

Resources

"Take Care When Giving Medications to Children," "Keeping Medications Safe: Prescription Tips for Parents," and "Medications in the Wrong Hands Can Be Hazardous," from the National Association of Retail Druggists; (703) 683-8200.

Nonprescription Medicines: What's Right For You?, from the Nonprescription Drug Manufacturers Association. To obtain a copy, send a SASE to

NDMA Publications Dept., 1150 Connecticut Ave. N.W., Washington, D.C. 20036.

A Parent's Guide to Proper Dosing from Tylenol; (800) 962-5357.

"Accidental Acetaminophen Overdoses," *Pediatrics for Parents,* volume 16, number 2; (207) 942-6212; richs@me.sdi.agate.net.

A Parent's Guide to Household Medicines and Child Safety, from Proctor and Gamble; (800) 844-3279.

"Poisoning," from the National Safe Kids Campaign; (202) 884-4993.

"Poisoning and Drugs: Find the Poisons in Your Home Before Your Child Does," from the Alisa Ann Ruch Burn Foundation and the Los Angeles Regional Drug and Poison Information Center.

NOISE

If your child is old enough for you to have uttered the words, "Turn down that stereo!" then it might be time to concern yourself with preserving her hearing. Noise-induced hearing loss, while it is usually a gradual and painless process, is also permanent. When a sound is too loud and/or goes on for too long, the tiny hairs in the inner ear give out, and cannot be repaired or replaced.

The loudness of a sound is measured in decibels, and to give you a basis for comparison, normal conversation measures around 60 dB. Many other sounds familiar to your child, however, are a lot louder.

Rock Concerts—120 to 130 dB

According to Hearing Education and Awareness for Rockers, a group of musicians and health professionals that advocates for noise awareness among the concert crowd, concert noise averages between 110 and 120 dB, and sound becomes painful at about 125 dB. The Occupational Safety and Health Administration (OSHA) says maximum safe exposure time for sounds at this level is 7.5 minutes or less.

What's worse, the decibel level can climb as high as 140 near the speakers (the equivalent of a gun going off next to your ear). This means the better the kids' seats, the greater your worries. But rather than take away their tickets, Dr. James L. Phillips, M.D., of Baylor College of Medicine in Houston, Texas, recommends some preventive action:

- Try to convince your kids to wear earplugs at concerts. There are lots of brands marketed to teens in Day-Glo colors, etc.
- Have them make occasional trips outside during their show to give their ears a break.
- If they notice a ringing in their ears or a "full" sensation, they should leave the concert immediately. This means damage is occurring.

If the kids won't listen to you, maybe someone they already listen to can help. Hook them up with HearNet, the Web site of Hearing Education and Awareness for Rockers. They'll find information on how to protect their ears, as well as testimonials from people like Pete Townshend and musicians from other groups you may not have heard of. They can click onto interviews with cool bands, concert information, and even order earplugs. The address is http://www.hearnet.com.

Stereos and Headsets—115 to 120 dB

Stereos and headsets played too loud can be just as damaging as a rock concert—only worse. Your child doesn't need front-row seats to wreck his hearing this way, and headsets mask the sound so that you can't tell exactly where the volume is set. The extended exposure to loud music these devices provide makes them a leading cause of hearing loss.

- Make your child keep his/her portable headset volume below level four. If you can hear the music when he's walking by, it is too loud.
- Insist that all stereos in your home be kept at a level where conversation can easily be heard. If you have to shout over the music, it is too loud.
- The same goes for the car stereo, no matter who is driving.

Firecrackers and children's toys—160 dB

A firecracker going off ten feet away has a decibel level of 160, and can damage hearing after only a onetime exposure. (See "Fireworks.") Cap guns and other toys are also a hazard, according to the American Academy of Pediatrics. CPSC regulations limit the decibel level of caps to no more than 158, but hearing damage occurs in just minutes at this level.

Other children's toys that make a lot of noise could also be a hazard (to your nerves as well as their ears). When buying your child a particularly loud toy, test it yourself first. Hold the toy beside your ear, and if the sound it makes is uncomfortably loud, it's time to either get a quieter toy, or make some rules about how close to the ears and how often the toy is to be used. (See "Toys.")

Hear the warnings

If you have doubts about your child's hearing, there are warning signs that can help you determine whether damage is occurring:

- Ringing or buzzing in the ears, or slight muffling of sounds
- Frequently failing to respond when called
- Misunderstanding of or inattentiveness to conversation
- Asking you to repeat words
- Incorrectly answering questions
- Cannot locate the source of a sound

• Turns one side of the head toward the speaker, or is continually turning up the volume on the television or stereo

You may think this sounds like typical preadolescent behavior, but if you answered yes to more than two of these questions, your child's hearing should probably be checked by an audiologist. Make an appointment today, and try to determine the source of the damage so that further injury can be prevented.

Resources

HearNet, the Web site of Hearing Education Awareness for Rockers; http://www.hearnet.com
"Now Hear This—About Headsets," by Jane Bowen, *Pediatrics for Parents*, volume 16, number 4.
"Teenagers Damaging Their Hearing," by James L. Phillips, M.D., "Health Focus," column from Baylor College of Medicine, Houston, Texas.

PACIFIERS

The only thing more maddening than a screaming infant is being unable to find the pacifier that will make the screaming stop. But parents' most common solution to this problem—tying the binky around baby's neck—sometimes kills babies.

Rule number one concerning pacifier safety is: **Never tie a pacifier or other object around your baby's neck**. Children can get these strings or ribbons caught on cribs, toys, pieces of furniture, and even doorknobs, and choke to death. You shouldn't tie pacifiers to children's clothing, toys, or any other object, either, because if a string is long enough to reach your child's mouth, it is probably long enough to be wrapped around his neck.

Buy only pacifiers that have large, strong shields to keep the baby from putting the whole pacifier in her mouth and choking on it. The shield should also have ventilation holes, just in case. And match the pacifier to the child. Some pacifiers are designed only for infants under three months old and are too small to be used by an older child.

Never substitute a bottle nipple for a pacifier. These nipples don't have a safety shield, and your baby could easily suck them into her throat and choke on them.

Pacifier Inspection

Before giving a pacifier to your baby, give it a quick safety inspection:

- Hold the nipple up to the light and check it for holes, tears, swelling, and signs of excessive wear. Then rub it between your fingers to see if it feels tacky. Most children put their pacifiers to pretty good use, and these signs of age could mean pieces of the nipple could crumble off and be swallowed by the baby.
- Make sure the shield is intact, and not cracked.
- Take the nipple in one hand and the shield in the other, and pull as hard as you can to make sure the nipple won't come off in your baby's mouth and choke her.

Get in the habit of performing this quick check every time you hand your child a pacifier, and retire any binky that fails inspection.

Resources _____

"Safe and Sound for Baby" from the Juvenile Products Manufacturers Association, 2 Greentree Centre, Box 955, Marlton, NJ 08053.

The Safe Nursery Buyer's Guide, and "Tips for Your Baby's Safety," from the U.S. Consumer Product Safety Commission; (800) 638-2772.

"What Every Parent, Relative & Child Care Provider Should Know About Pacifier Safety," from Evenflo; (800) 356-BABY.

PARENTS' BEDROOM

You may think your bedroom belongs to *you*. After all, that's where you put most of the stuff that is truly and personally yours, and that you don't want anyone else to get into.

Well, now that you are a parent, you must treat every room in your house as if it belongs to *the kids*—or at least as if you expect them to find their way in there eventually. This means taking an extra look around at all those things you don't want anybody to get into, and making doubly sure nobody can. Your common sense will probably serve as an adequate guide in this endeavor, but I'll list a few things to get you started:

- *Your dry cleaning,* or more specifically, the plastic bags that encase it, is big-time bad news, because the CPSC says that at least fifteen children a year suffocate on plastic bags. Tear 'em off, tie them in a knot, and throw them away. You should also toss away any pins or other sharp metal objects your dry cleaner has thought to include.
- *Your jewelry box* is full of shiny, pointy, and attractive things that just might end up in a toddler's throat or wrapped around her neck. Put it up high and, if your child is especially interested, out of sight.

- *Your bedside table* just might contain a handy bottle of aspirin, sleeping pills, antacids, or other medications. (See "Medicines.") Or maybe you have a framed photograph under (breakable) glass or a bunch of loose change. These things are better kept elsewhere.
- *Makeup* and other beauty essentials such as curling irons, perfume, hair spray, hairpins, rollers, blow dryers—you name it— could create an ugly accident. Talc in face powder could damage your child's lungs if inhaled, hair spray in the eyes could permanently impair vision, and even something as innocent looking as a lipstick could be bitten off and choked on by a toddler.
- *Electrical cords and outlets* might be left unguarded in rooms where children aren't expected to be. (See "Electrical Outlets/ Cords.")
- *Window cords* should be kept out of reach. (See "Windows.")
- *Check your dresser* for any small objects your child could choke on, or for things that might coax your child into climbing up the drawers. Put these temptations out of sight. Test the knobs to make sure they cannot be pulled out and choked on. Finally, give the top of the dresser a good yank to make sure it can't be tipped over if your child does decide to go climbing. If the dresser tips, try weighing down the bottom drawers with some heavy objects.

Resources

"Room-by-room Childproofing Guide," *Healthy Kids Birth–3*, from the American Academy of Pediatrics.

"Dresser Safety Alert," from the U.S. Consumer Product Safety Commission; (800) 638-2772.

PARTIES (GROWN-UP)

Before my husband and I were parents, we rarely encountered children at parties and seldom had them as guests at our parties. But as our circle of friends began to be fruitful and multiply, they started bringing their kids along—and eventually so did we.

I like the idea of taking children to adult gatherings when appropriate. But because these functions are meant to center around the adults, they may be hazardous to children whose parents aren't prepared. "Adults are engaged in social situations with one another, and no one has direct responsibility for the children," says Dr. Christine Wood of Failure Analysis Associates, a consulting firm that investigates causes of accidents and injuries. And children left to run around together may be occupied and out of the way, but they can also cook up a lot more ways to get into trouble.

Cigarettes and cigarette butts are one of the major causes of party injuries, both from burns during accidental contact and from kids eating them. Other dangers include alcohol poisoning from unfinished drinks left within reach—especially those mixed with orange or tomato juice or punch. Less than half a cup of a mixed drink could be lethal to a child. Hot drinks also cause a lot of scald burns.

If it's your party, keep in mind the ages of any children who will be attending. Are they older than yours? Younger? You may need to do a little extra babyproofing to make the house safe for your smallest guests. Wood also recommends hiring a babysitter to keep the kids safely occupied and give the adults time to enjoy the party.

If you are attending a party with your spouse, take turns being responsible for the children, either with each other, or with other parents attending the party. Don't expect that your host, even one with children, has babyproofed to fit your child's needs. Scout the terrain early in the evening for trouble spots. Then you can either keep the kid out of the area in question or move a few hazardous or breakable objects to higher ground.

And it never hurts to bring a good video the kids can watch. The other parents at the party will thank you.

PETS

A pet can be a wonderful companion to the entire family—especially to a child. In my view, there is no better way to learn about unconditional love and caring. But children can be scratched, bitten, or worse if they aren't taught proper pet safety.

Whether you are teaching your child about your old friend Fido or bringing a new pet into the home, it's your job to supervise your child's encounters with the family pet and teach them how to care for their animal friends safely.

Picking a pet

Even if they already have one or more animals at home, parents often want to get their kids a pet that is "their own." The responsibility of caring for a pet, however, is generally more than a child under seventeen or eighteen can handle reliably, according to Leslie Sinclair, DVM, director of companion animal care for the Humane Society of the United States. This means Mom and Dad should plan to do a good portion of the loving and caring themselves. "You never obtain a pet for a child," explains Sinclair. "The pet has to be a commitment the parents have made."

This means that in selecting a pet for their child, the parents have to take into account their own lifestyle and personality as well, according to Ben Hart, DVM, Ph.D., and chief of behavior service at the School of Veterinary Medicine at the University of California, Davis.

Not recommended

Most traditional pets can be good companions for children as long as proper safety rules are followed. But Sinclair doesn't recommend nondomesticated animals such as hedgehogs, ferrets, or other exotic animals du jour, for kids—even though you may find one at your local pet store, where you will be told they make great pets. "You can't expect a wild animal not to be wild," says Sinclair, explaining that even animals that have been in people's homes for years might revert to their natural behavior and bite or scratch a child. And these animals are virtually impossible to care for humanely, which doesn't teach good lessons about compassion or kindness.

Sinclair and the U.S. Centers for Disease Control also warn against reptiles of any kind as pets for children—especially children under age five. These animals carry salmonella, which is highly contagious and could be deadly in small children. Even babies who have had no contact with the pet can become infected through contact with someone else who has handled the reptile or cleaned its cage.

You should also make sure there are no pet reptiles in your child's school or day-care center, or in the home of anyone caring for a child under age five. The bacteria that cause the illness are easily spread and difficult to control.

Dogs and cats

Dogs and cats are among the top pets recommended by Sinclair. Just make sure the animal you choose has a kid-friendly personality and has been properly socially adapted.

Traits to look for in a breed of family dog include playfulness and demand for affection, says Hart, who coauthored *The Perfect Puppy: How to Choose Your Dog by Its Behavior*. Hart explains that around a child, you also want a breed that's not too aggressive or territorial, and isn't easily provoked into snapping at children. In *Perfect Puppy,* Hart ranks many breeds of dog according to these and other traits. If you're looking to bring a canine into your life, I recommend getting your hands on a copy.

Dogs and cats of any breed need to be exposed to whatever conditions they are expected to adapt to—be it walks along a busy street or small children—between eight and sixteen weeks of age. Hart recommends getting a puppy or a kitten so you can acclimate them yourself. This also allows you to visit the breeder and observe the behavior of the parents—a good indication of what you can expect when the animal grows up. Hart recommends extreme caution in choosing a puppy from a breeder who is reluctant to let your child play with the mother dog. "That should be a warning," he explains.

If you've missed the window (you got the dog or cat before the baby), some animals will still adapt, but parents should take extra care when introducing them to children.

There are also good reasons to consider adopting an older dog or cat. "An eight-week-old kitten is not a good pet for a two-year-old," says Sinclair, explaining that a kitten of this age might react to a small child's clumsy handling by biting or scratching. "And they're very hard to fix if you break them," she adds. "With very tiny children, you might want to look for an older animal who has [experience with kids]."

This means you'll need to find out about the animal's background. The person supplying the pet, whether a pet-store owner, the animal's previous owner, or an employee of a shelter, should be able to help. There are also books on the subject, such as *The Second-Hand Dog,* by Carol Lee Benjamin.

Some breeds of dog—rottweilers or pit bulls, for example—may not be recommended because they are very powerful and "could do a lot of damage if they decided to harm a child." However, it is important to keep in mind that every animal is an individual.

"Know as much as you can about that breed, and then know as much as you can about that animal," advises Sinclair.

Fish and birds

Fish and birds cannot be cuddled, but they still require lots of care and attention, and can be fascinating to watch. If your child is content just to watch, they're great. "A view-only pet is OK for a child as long as the child understands that," explains Sinclair. But if your child craves a cuddly pet, forget the fish.

Rodents

All types of rodents can make good kid pets, according to Sinclair, whose personal favorites are guinea pigs, but they must be socialized the same way a cat or a dog would, or they won't be eager to be handled and might bite. This means the pet store might not be the best place to purchase a hamster, rat, or guinea pig, since these animals are not usually individually socialized. A better bet is to check with your local shelter. Larger shelters adopt out small mammals and will have some information on the animal's age and background.

Rabbits can also make great pets, but not usually before your child is seven or eight years old. According to the House Rabbit Society, an organization dedicated to the adoption and care of bunnies, these long-eared rodents don't like to be held and are delicate animals that might be hurt by young children. This will make it tough for a young child to play with a bunny, and the child may lose interest.

Rabbits also require a great deal of space, since the society recommends letting your rabbit live indoors, with as much out-of-cage time as possible. This means they also require toilet training and "bunny-proofing", much like a two-year-old child.

If you have a very young child, keep in mind that the smaller rodents are fast and frail, and might not be safe for them to handle. If they don't lose or hurt the animal, it might bite or scratch out of fear. The same holds true for rabbits. For small children, you want a large breed of rabbit, which can stand up to more hugging and petting.

Pet pointers

No matter what type of furred, feathered, or finned friend shares your home, things will be more civilized if you teach the family the law of the jungle.

- If you're getting an animal you have no experience with, do your homework. Find out as much as you can about how the animal will behave and what it needs to be happy. Then teach your kids about the animal so that they understand and respect the animal's behavior.
- Whatever animal you choose, make it a part of the family, not a part of the landscape. This will keep your pet cleaner, healthier, and better socialized. "A dog that is kept tied out in the backyard is more likely to jump on or bite a child," says Sinclair. "It is more likely to be dirty, and more likely to have fleas." The same holds true for cats who stay outdoors, and even rabbits. Caged animals, even though they are in the house, will tend to bite if they are not let out or handled often.
- Children need to be supervised when playing with their animal, and playtime is best scheduled when the child is in a calm, relaxed mood.
- Make and enforce rules against hitting, teasing, chasing, tail pulling, etc. If pushed far enough, most animals will respond by biting or scratching. An estimated 2.8 million children were bitten by dogs in 1995, according to the Humane Society of the United States, and this is often because they have not been taught the right way to interact with animals.

    To prevent these behaviors, spend a lot of time showing your child "good" ways to interact with their pet. Try to catch your child when she is about to act in the wrong way, and redirect her. If your child refuses to stop doing something that will hurt or scare the pet, keep them separated for a "time-out."

- Have a place where the animal can go to be by itself when it is tired of playing, and teach your child to respect the animal's right to take a rest. Make it a rule that they should not disturb the dog in her bed, or the cat if he has run under the sofa. An animal that has been pushed too far may bite or scratch.
- Take care when feeding an animal. Some dogs and even cats become territorial around their food dish. A dog or cat eager for a treat may accidentally scratch or knock over a child in an attempt to get at the food. A rodent being hand-fed may accidentally bite.
- Teach your child proper hygiene during pet care. Kids should wash their hands after playing with, feeding, or grooming their pet, or after cleaning its cage or litter box. Diseases that can be transmitted between the pet and your child include internal worms (from kittens or puppies), rabies (from dogs and cats), skin diseases such as ringworm (from dogs and cats), and salmonella (from reptiles).

You should also take good care of the animal, bathing it if recommended, and taking it for regular veterinary checkups and vaccinations. Even rodents should go to the vet once or twice a year.

If you go about things the right way, your pets can coexist safely and happily with your child. And your child just might make a new and important friend.

Resources

"Rabbits and Children," by Carolyn Mixon, from the House Rabbit Society; (510) 521-4631.

"Fad News Is Bad News," by Richard H. Farinato and Rachel A. Lamb, *Humane Society of the United States News,* Fall 1995.

The Perfect Puppy: How to Choose Your Dog by Its Behavior, by Benjamin
  L. Hart and Lynette A. Hart (W. H. Freeman and Company).

PLANTS

If your little darling decides eating her greens means a few bites of
the philodendron, she could be in for a trip to the emergency
room, so you need to know a bit more about your houseplants
than whether or not you can keep them alive.

Know what you sow

Parents should know the names of all plants in and around their
home so they know what to tell the hospital or poison control center if they find their child eating something he shouldn't, according
to Frances Weindler, a supervisor at the Los Angeles Regional Drug
and Poison Information Center since 1959. "You'd be amazed at
how many calls we get where people tell us, 'My child just ate red
berries from a green bush,'" she says. "And we can't give those people any answers."

Identifying the plants around you also gives you a chance to get
rid of the more toxic varieties, or at least make sure plant and child
are kept apart.

You can identify unknown plants by taking a piece of the plant,
or the whole plant if possible, to a nursery. Get both the botanical
and the colloquial or common name of the plant so it will be easier to look up in reference books, suggests Weindler. Once you
have the name, you can find out whether the plant is toxic by calling your local poison control center. The number should be in the
white pages of your telephone directory under "Poison Control
Center."

The oxalates

The philodendron is one of the most common poisonous plants found in the home, says Weindler, "because they have so many species of it [around 70], and because it grows so nicely." These are members of a group of toxic plants called oxalates, which contain irritating substances called ocalate salts in the sap. Biting into the plant can cause burning, swelling, and pain. Dumbcane, or dieffenbachia, is another common household plant in this group.

Contact with oxalates usually causes a child's lips and mouth to swell, and may even cause enough swelling around the vocal cords to prevent the child from talking. This irritation could make it difficult for the child to swallow or breathe. However, children don't usually ingest the plant. "Usually children, when they get a taste of it, drop it right away because of the burning sensation," says Weindler.

Other oxalates: arrowhead vine, begonia, Boston ivy, caladium, cala lily, Chinese evergreen, elephant's ear, mother-in-law plant, nephthytis, pothos, schefflera, umbrella trees.

Toxic or potentially toxic plants

Castor-bean plants and oleanders are two of the most common toxic plants found around people's gardens, according to Weindler. These plants can cause a wide range of internal problems, from mild irritation to severe organ damage.

Other toxic to potentially toxic plants: African lily, agapanthus, aloe, aloe vera, azalea, bird of paradise, boxwood, chinaberry, creeping charlie, cyclamen, daffodil, diathus, foxglove, heart ivy, heavenly bamboo, holly (most common around Christmas), hyacinth, ivy, juniper, lily of the Nile, lily of the valley, lobelia, majesty, mistletoe (another holiday favorite), morning glory, needlepoint ivy, nightshade, parlor ivy, periwinkle, pyracantha, rhododendron, rosary bead, Shasta daisy, spider mum, string of pearls.

Plants that cause dermatitis

Ficus trees are a nice way to bring the outdoors in, but can cause an unpleasant skin reaction in children who come in contact with the sap. The ficus, and other plants like it can cause skin rashes, itching, and irritation.

Other plants that cause dermatitis: African lily, agapanthus, aloe, aloe vera, boxwood, cactus, caladium, candytuft, elephant's ear, fiddleleaf fig, heart ivy, hyacinth, ivy, juniper, lily of the Nile, marigold, mother-in-law plant, needlepoint ivy, parlor ivy, philodendron, pothos, rubber tree, schefflera, Shasta daisy, spider mum, umbrella tree.

Unknown plants

Some species of plants have not been extensively studied, but some of the available information indicates they might possibly be toxic. These should also be avoided.

They include gardenias, grape ivy, mother-in-law tongue, pansy, poinsettia, pot mum, and sweet pea.

Other types of plants that might be dangerous are those with especially velvety leaves or flowers (such as African violets). "Sometimes a plant is completely nontoxic, but might get stuck at the back of the throat," explains Weindler. In fact, if you discover your child chewing on a plant, check to make sure the plant is not lodged in the throat before you call for help.

The next step in administering first aid is usually to rinse the child's mouth and give them cool fluids such as water or milk to dilute the plant's toxic elements in the stomach. Wash any areas where the skin might have come into contact with the plant with cool water and mild soap. In the case of toxic plants or those that produce a severe skin reaction, call the poison control center or your doctor.

Green but wise

The L.A. Poison Control Center recommends keeping most plants, seeds and bulbs out of children's reach and teaching your children not to put plants or plant parts into their mouths. Weindler adds that children often chew on plants because they see an adult doing it, so avoid this practice.

If you have plants in your yard that can cause dermatitis, or if you are hiking or walking in an area that does, teach your children to avoid them. If your child does come in contact with an unknown plant, keep him from rubbing his eyes. And make sure he knows that the only plants you want him chewing on are those he finds on his dinner plate.

Resources

"Plants . . . Beautiful But May Be Toxic!", from the Los Angeles Regional Drug and Poison Information Center; (800) 777-6476.

PLAYGROUNDS

Looking for a hazard-free place to "park" your child? The National Recreation and Park Association says 170,000 children a year are seriously injured in playground accidents—some fatally—so take your child's playground seriously.

It is important to let kids play and explore, as long as you are sure that what they are exploring is safe. First scout out the terrain, looking for hazardous equipment and unsavory characters—any-one hanging around the park who looks suspicious. When evalu-

ating playground conditions, trust your instincts. If it looks dangerous, it probably is.

If your child is injured on the playground, there is a 70 percent
chance that the injury will be the result of a fall, so make sure the
play area offers something soft to land on, such as rubber mats,
mulch, or sand. You shouldn't find concrete, blacktop, packed
earth, or even grass within six feet in all directions of anything your
child is likely to climb on. If the protective surface is mulch or sand,
make sure it isn't worn or compacted. The "fall zone" at the exit area
of a slide should extend four feet farther than the height of the slide,
while swings require a fall zone of twice their height in front and behind, and six feet to the side. Make sure equipment is properly
spaced. There should be a minimum of twelve feet between pieces
of stationary play equipment so there is room for children to circu-
late and so they will not strike one piece if they fall off another.

Inspect each piece of equipment carefully, looking for bolt ends
or other sharp pieces that could harm your child—S-type hooks,
handholds that protrude outward from a support structure—or
moving parts on suspension bridges, merry-go-rounds, or seesaws
that could pinch or crush a child's finger. Make sure there are no
broken or missing parts or peeling paint and that all pieces seem
secure, with no apparent signs of loosening.

Next, crouch down to your child's level and look for trip hazards
like exposed concrete footings, tree roots, or garden borders. And
make sure there are no openings on playground equipment that
would let a child's body pass through, but trap his or her head
(generally between 3 1/2 and 9 inches), or elevated surfaces such
as platforms, ramps or bridges without guardrails.

The Consumer Product Safety Commission recommends that
heavy swings such as animal-figure or multiple-occupancy types,
free-swinging ropes, and swinging exercise rings not be used on
public playgrounds.

Last but not least, keep your eyes peeled, because lack of supervision is a contributing factor in 40 percent of playground acci-

dents. The kids may be busy at the monkey bars, but this is no time for you to sit in the shade and read a book. Watch what your children are doing, making sure they are using the equipment properly and that they aren't attempting any feats beyond their abilities. Many playgrounds have a separate yard for younger children, but once again, safety is really a matter of common sense. You know what your child is capable of doing. If you see your three-year-old climbing to the top of a slide taller than the downtown skyline, you have to decide whether to make her come down or to stand behind the ladder and make sure she reaches the top safely, then race to the slide exit to guarantee a soft landing.

Use this checklist from the National Playground Safety Institute to evaluate your favorite slide and swing sanctuary, and watch out for the "Dirty Dozen:"

- *Improper protective surfacing* under play equipment, the leading cause of playground injuries, includes concrete, blacktop, packed earth and grass. (A twelve-inch depth of wood chips, sand, or synthetic rubber mats are safer.)
- *Inadequate fall zones* where the protective surfacing extends less than six feet in all directions from stationary play equipment or the exit area of a slide, or two times a swing's height in front and behind and six feet to the side of the structure.
- *Bolt ends, hooks, protruding handholds* or other objects capable of impaling or cutting a child, or catching on clothing.
- *Openings between 3 1/2 and 9 inches wide,* which allow a child's body to pass through but entrap the head.
- *Insufficient equipment spacing* or overlapping fall zones on equipment more than twenty-four inches high.
- *Trip hazards* like exposed concrete footings, abrupt surface elevation changes, tree roots, stumps, and rocks.
- *Lack of supervision,* which contributes to more than 40 percent of playground injuries.
- *Age-inappropriate activities.*

- *Lack of maintenance.*
- *Components that could cut skin,* or parts of moving equipment that could crush or pinch a child's finger.
- *Platforms with no guardrails* if they are higher than twenty inches.
- *Equipment not recommended* for public playgrounds, such as heavy swings, free-swinging ropes, and exercise rings or trapeze bars.

The Great Indoors

Indoor play equipment is becoming as common as backyard swing sets at malls, fast-food restaurants, and indoor play centers, with more than 7,600 places to play at last count. In March of 1996, the U.S. Consumer Product Safety Commission deemed these centers "safe alternatives to traditional, outdoor playgrounds."

But, as always, adult supervision is a big part of the equation. So you should watch for:

- Slides that exit into ball pools, or climbing equipment located in ball pools. (Children coming down the slide or jumping off the equipment can injure other children in the ball pool. A thirteen-year-old boy was killed this way in 1995.)
- Tears in the safety netting or cargo webbing and rope equipment. (This could allow children to climb onto the outer part of the equipment, or become trapped in the netting.)
- Tears in the flooring surface (a tripping hazard).
- General cleanliness (which means the operator is performing routine maintenance).
- Posted safety guidelines (which should be obeyed by your children and others).
- Use and size recommendations (which keep smaller children away from their older, rougher counterparts).
- Loose clothing and jewelry (a strangulation hazard).

- Children playing at the base of slides or climbing equipment, or climbing up the front of a slide.

The Home-court advantage

Having play equipment in your own backyard means you know the terrain, but there are still a few safety rules to follow.

- Make sure your yard is large enough to accommodate the equipment you are considering. The site should allow you to easily see and supervise the kids at all times.
- Don't place the equipment too close to fences, trees, utility poles and wires, or any other obstacles that could injure your child.
- Purchase only equipment that meets ASTM F1148 Safety Standards for Home Play Equipment.
- Make sure the equipment is installed and anchored to meet manufacturer's specifications, and is level and well drained.
- Allow for proper fall zones around your equipment, and cover the surrounding area with something soft for the kids to fall on.

Resources

"The Dirty Dozen: Are They Hiding in Your Child's Playground?", from the National Recreation and Parks Association; (703) 820-4940.

Handbook for Public Playground Safety and "CPSC Report Confirms Safety of Soft Contained Playgrounds," from the U.S. Consumer Product Safety Commission; (800) 638-2772.

"CPSC and Manufacturers Alert Playgrounds to Remove Animal Swings," from the U.S. Consumer Product Safety Commission.

"Home Playground Safety Tips," from the National Recreation and Park Association.

PLAYPENS

A playpen can be a helpful way to ensure your baby's safety when there are other demands on your attention. But like any device that would seem to free a parent from the duty of constant supervision (walkers, high chairs, bath seats, infant seats), playpens can be dangerous if used incorrectly.

About two thousand children a year go to the emergency room because of accidents involving playpens, according to the Consumer Product Safety Commission, which offers the following advice:

Mesh playpens

- The mesh should have small weave, with openings no larger than one-quarter inch. The baby could get tangled in the openings of looser-weave mesh.
- The mesh should be securely attached to the top and the floor of the playpen, with no tears, holes, loose threads, or loose staples. Babies have strangled in holes or loose threads in their playpens.
- The vinyl- or fabric-covered top rail of the playpen should be in good shape, with no holes or tears. A teething child could bite off a piece of the material and choke.
- The drop sides should be up, and securely locked in place, whenever a baby is in the playpen. When the side is left down, it forms a pocket of loose mesh that could trap a baby's face against the mattress. Babies have suffocated when they fell into this loose pocket of mesh.

Wooden playpens

- The spaces between the slats of a wooden playpen should be no greater than 2 3/8 inches wide. A baby could become trapped between slats with larger spaces.

- The wooden parts of the playpen should be smooth and free from splinters, and all parts should be securely attached.
- If the playpen was made before 1978, test the paint to make sure it contains no lead.

Playing it safe

- Don't put large toys or bumper pads into the playpen with the baby. They could be used to climb out, causing a dangerous fall to the floor.
- Never tie toys or other items across the top of a playpen, and don't hang them from the sides. A baby could get tangled in the string and strangle.
- If you are putting an infant to sleep in a playpen, remove any large stuffed animals or heavy blankets that could cover her face and suffocate her.

I also recommend that you try to be in the same room with any child who is left in a playpen. Being there is your surest guarantee that your baby is safe. If you must be out of the room, pop in frequently to make sure everything is okay.

Resources

Safe & Sound for Baby: A Guide to Baby-Product Safety, Use, and Selection, from the Juvenile Product Manufacturers Association, 2 Greentree Centre, Box 955, Marlton, NJ 08053.

"Tips for Your Baby's Safety" and *The Safe Nursery: A Booklet to Help Avoid Injuries from Nursery Furniture and Equipment,* from the U.S. Consumer Product Safety Commission; (800) 638-2772.

RADON

Radon is an all-natural, invisible, odorless gas that can harm your family. The fact that this is not a man-made threat (like carbon monoxide or lead) shouldn't fool you into taking it less seriously. In fact, radon is the second leading cause of lung cancer in the United States (after smoking) according to the U.S. surgeon general. The U.S. Environmental Protection Agency estimates that one in fifteen U.S. homes—new and old—have high levels of radon.

This gas full of radioactive particles comes from underground uranium deposits, seeping into homes through cracks in the foundation and around water and sewer pipes. *Consumer Reports* calls it "a significant concern for homeowners who use their finished basements often," but says most apartment dwellers need not worry about exposure, since radon doesn't often reach much above the ground floor.

Unlike carbon monoxide, there are no preventive measures you can take to keep radon levels down, and no symptoms that will warn you that you are being exposed. The only way to know if you have a radon problem is by using a radon test kit, which should cost you between ten and thirty-five dollars at most hardware stores.

Testing for radon is especially important in homes with children, as their systems more readily absorb toxins such as radiation.

Test kits come in two types—long-term and short-term. Short-term kits usually test radon levels over a seven-day period, while longer-term units give an average reading for periods of ninety days or longer. Because radon levels fluctuate significantly from day to day, *Consumer Reports* suggests using a long-term kit to obtain a more accurate reading.

Besides being inexpensive, these testers are easy to use. You just open the device and leave it undisturbed in the lowest occupied living area. Then you seal up the unit and mail it off to the manufacturer's lab to get your results, which could take anywhere between four days and a month.

If your results show a serious problem, it can cost an average of $1,000 to $1,500 to fix, according to the Environmental Protection Agency. To find someone qualified to fix the problem, make sure your contractor is certified by the EPA's Radon Contractor Proficiency program and by your state, if it has a licensing program. For help in locating a contractor and more information, call the National Safety Council Radon Hotline at (800) 767-7236. For more detailed information about radon itself, visit the U.S. Geological Survey Radon Web site at http://sedwww.cr.usgs.gov:8080/radon-home.html.

Resources

The National Safety Council Radon Helpline; (800) 55-RADON.
"Reducing Radon Risks," "Consumer's Guide to Radon," and "A Citizen's Guide to Radon," from the U.S. Environmental Protection Agency.
"Radon: Worth Learning About," *Consumer Reports,* July 1995, pp. 464-465. Reprints available. Write to CU/Reprints, 101 Truman Ave., Yonkers, NY 10703-1057.

SCHOOL

Parents are rightly concerned about the quality of education their child receives at school. But these concerns are sometimes displaced by worries about their child's physical safety. Children can be injured or even killed on the way to school or while on campus. And kids are often victims of bullying or violent crimes at school.

Getting there

Parents have more to worry about than getting their kids to school on time. They also need to make sure they get there safely, and unless you are driving them yourself, it means teaching kids the rules of the road.

The walk: Making your children's walk to school safe starts by teaching them basic pedestrian safety.

- Walk on the sidewalk, not in the street. If there is no sidewalk, walk on the left side of the street, facing traffic. Avoid alleys or cutting across yards, because drivers might not see you.
- Walk with a friend, if you can.
- Don't run. If you trip or drop something, you could be hit by a car.
- Obey traffic signals, and always look before you cross the street—even if the light is green. (Drivers don't always obey the signals, and may run the light.)
- Look left, right, and left again whenever you cross a street. (See also "Street Safety.")

But it may take more than safe habits to make sure your child makes it to school. One in eight students in the 1993 National Crime Survey reported being afraid they would be attacked going to and from school. If your child is afraid to walk to school because of a gang or bully, take these concerns seriously. Help them find a safe route to school, or drive them there if you have to. Organize a carpool in your neighborhood, or a group of parents to patrol the street and make sure the kids are safe when walking to school.

It is also a good idea to have your child keep to the same one or two routes to and from school. This way, if she is late or missing, you'll have a good idea of where to start looking.

The carpool: Know who's driving your children, whether it be the parent or grandparent of one of their friends, or a pal's older brother or sister. Make sure that person knows and enforces car safety rules. (See "Car Safety.") And make sure your child knows that the driver is in charge, and should be obeyed if he or she asks for quiet in the car or tells the kids to buckle up.

The bus: The wheels on the bus take 23 million children a day to school. And every year, forty-five of those children are killed, according to a 1996 study at the Connecticut Children's Medical Center.

Most buses carrying children to school do not have seat belts, but few of the children killed in school-bus accidents are passengers on the bus, according to the American Academy of Pediatrics. The academy still recommends installing seat belts on all school buses, but the cost involved keeps most school districts from cooperating.

More important than doing battle with your district over the installation of belts is teaching your child good bus safety habits and making sure there is proper adult supervision on the bus (besides the driver) to enforce safety rules. While on the bus, kids should stay seated, keep the noise level to a minimum so the driver can concentrate, use seat belts if they are provided, and keep their hands, arms, and heads inside the bus.

But your child needs to be even more careful getting on and off the bus than when riding it. Ninety percent of children killed in school-bus accidents are run over by their own buses while they are waiting for the bus, or getting on or off, according to Connecticut Children's Medical Center.

The National Highway Traffic Safety Administration recommends the following precautions for students:

- Stop, look left, right, then left again before crossing any street on the way to the bus stop.
- Walk along the side of the street at least ten feet ahead of the bus before crossing the street in front of a bus.
- Stand well back from the street when lined up to wait for a bus, and wait until the bus has completely stopped, the door is open,

and the driver has signaled that it is okay before walking toward the bus. A great way to help reduce accidents is to talk your school board into painting stencils on the sidewalks at bus stops to show kids where to stand. Researchers at Connecticut Children's Hospital estimate that these stencils could cut the amount of unsafe behavior in half.

- Use the handrails when climbing the stairs.
- Be careful that clothes or backpacks don't get caught in the bus doors or handrail when getting on or off. Kids with trapped clothing could be dragged under the bus and run over.
- Walk three giant steps away from the bus as soon as they get off.

The lay of the land

When visiting your child's school, check out the playground she will be using. It should contain age-appropriate equipment that is kept in good repair. Grass and shrubs should be neatly trimmed and sidewalks kept clear to prevent accidents, and there should be proper protective surfacing under slides, swings, and climbing structures. (See "Playgrounds.")

You should look for the same safety measures inside the facility as you would take in your home. Are walkways and stairways kept clear and well lit? Is everything clean and in good repair? Are toxic substances kept locked up? If the students use art or chemistry materials, are they age-appropriate and nontoxic?

Environmental factors

A school that appears completely safe could still have environmental hazards that endanger your child's health. If your child's school was built before the 1970s, it likely contains some asbestos building materials. These materials are considered safe if they are in good condition in low-traffic areas. But if the materials are worn and students are exposed, they could be increasing the children's chances of lung cancer and other diseases. The EPA estimates that about 44,900 U.S. schools contain asbestos. If you suspect your school has a problem, you can contact the EPA ombudsman in charge of helping citizens with school asbestos at (800) 368-5888. (See "Asbestos.")

Radon problems can happen anywhere, and this includes your child's school. The EPA recommends that all schools test for radon. Make sure yours has, and that any problems uncovered were dealt with correctly. (See "Radon.") The school should also have tested its water for lead, which can cause severe health problems—especially in young children. (See "Water.")

But probably the most pervasive environmental problem in schools is indoor air quality. The U.S. General Accounting Office reported to Congress in August of 1995 that nearly one in five schools reported indoor air problems, placing 8.3 million students in jeopardy. The problem is largely due to the number of students stuffed into each classroom. Current building standards assume seven people for every one thousand square feet of office space, but allow fifty students in the same area in schools.

This means schools should be bringing in lots of fresh air, but many keep buildings tightly sealed as an energy-saving measure. Money is also a factor when schools fail to upgrade air-conditioning and ventilation systems or deal with such problems as leaking roofs and windows promptly.

The solution is to reduce or eliminate known sources of indoor air pollution, such as toxic cleaning products used during school hours, carpets that harbor dust and mold, and chemicals used in student chemistry, photo, and art projects. The school must also keep the buildings and the existing ventilation system properly maintained. Air ducts should be cleaned and leaks repaired to prevent mold growth in walls and floors. Ventilation systems should be upgraded whenever possible. Letting students breathe easier keeps them in school and healthy—not home with the colds, allergies, or asthma that poor air quality can aggravate.

Emergency preparedness

Your child's school should have a written emergency and disaster policy that covers how the school will keep students safe in the event of whatever disaster is likely to occur in your part of the country. They should also teach a curriculum that helps students understand what will happen in the event of an emergency, and have practice drills so students clearly understand what to do. There should also be adequate emergency supplies on hand.

Find out what your school's policy is. If anything seems amiss, you can get more information about disaster planning in schools from the Federal Emergency Management Agency, P.O. Box 70274, Washington, D.C. 20024.

Your school should also be prepared for smaller emergencies. They should have emergency information on file for each student, including phone numbers of parents and others to contact. If there is no school nurse, there should at least be first-aid supplies on hand (see "First-Aid Kits") and someone who knows how to use them. There should be a clear, written procedure detailing what will be done if a student is seriously injured, including what hospital or emergency facility they will be taken to.

Supervision and security

Safety at school, as in all other areas, is often a matter of proper supervision. In 1994, a six-year-old girl in a Los Angeles area school was raped when she went alone to use the rest room during classes. In the wake of this horrifying incident, the district adopted a policy of sending students to the bathroom only in pairs.

While this particular type of violence may be rare on most campuses, students who are left unsupervised are also left vulnerable— no matter where they go to school. Lack of supervision means bullying and other types of unsafe behavior can go unchecked.

Campus violence

A theft or violent crime happens on or near our nation's schools every six seconds that school is in session, according to a 1993 report by the National School Safety Center. One of every twelve students has stayed away from school because they were afraid of getting hurt, and one in eleven students has said they were the victim of a crime at school.

Bullying is probably the most pervasive form of violence on campus. The National School Safety Center estimates that one child in ten is regularly attacked verbally or physically by bullies. If your child becomes withdrawn, abruptly loses interest in school, brings home lower-than-usual grades, or shows any signs of physical abuse, it may be a sign that he is the target of a bully.

You can't be at the school every day to protect your child, but you can bring your concerns to the attention of school officials. You should also keep your own written record of bullying incidents to submit to the school principal. Teach your child to try to steer clear of kids who bully them, and when confrontations arise, teach them how to handle them safely.

Your child needs to learn to be assertive, express feelings clearly, and stand up for herself verbally—but never physically—when confronted by a bully. This show of confidence is enough to discourage many bullies, who need to feel power over others. If a bully can't intimidate your child, he may find someone else to pick on. If a show of confidence isn't enough, and the situation becomes dangerous, teach your child to walk away and get help from an adult.

You can role-play these types of situations with your child to help him be prepared for trouble. You might also want to get your child involved in the martial arts, which teach confidence and self-defense over violence.

Gangs are another way that violence is spreading across our schools. According to the National PTA, gangs are spreading from urban areas into suburban and rural communities. Gang members can be as young as nine, says the American Psychological Association.

You can find out if there are active gangs in your community from your local police department, which probably has a gang prevention program in place. They can provide you with information about how to identify gang members and how to tell if your child has become involved with a gang.

The best way to keep your child out of gangs is to prevent the low self-esteem, academic failure, and boredom that often drives kids to join. Spend as much time as you can with your child. Know his friends and where they hang out. Set curfews and enforce them. And keep kids busy and involved with sports, clubs, volunteer work, and family activities. If your child is having trouble in school, do everything you can to help her. Be there when she does her homework; get a tutor; talk to the teacher. Kids without time on their hands have no time for gangs.

Organizing for change

No matter what types of safety problems you have found at your child's school, one of the best ways to solve them is to become involved yourself. One of the best books I've found on the subject of school safety, *Safe at School: Awareness and Action for Parents of Kids Grades K-12,* by Carol Silverman Saunders, recommends starting a parent safety group.

To get started, tell the principal about the group you would like to organize. Ask for permission to send a flyer home with the students that describes the group and tells interested parents whom they can contact to join.

Next, organize a regular meeting schedule and get a group consensus on which issues you will tackle first. Research the problem and find out all you can about it. Develop several possible solutions to the problem and meet with the principal to discuss them. Then choose one and carry it out.

If your solution doesn't work right away, modify it. If it does, you can move on to your next project. You'll find that with a little time, and the help of others, you can give yourself some peace of mind about your child's safety at school.

Resources _____

Safe at School: Awareness and Action for Parents of Kids Grades K-12, by Carol Silverman Saunders (Free Spirit, 1994).
"School Safety Update," from the National School Safety Center, September 1993; (805) 373-9977.
"Simple Sidewalk Stencil Could Save Children's Lives" and "School Bus Safety," from the American Academy of Pediatrics.
"Traffic Safety Outlook: School Bus Safety," from the National Highway Transportation Safety Administration.
Environmental Hazards in Your School, from the U.S. Environmental Protection Agency.
Safeguarding Your Children, from the National PTA and the Allstate Foundation.

SHOPPING: STORES AND MALLS

Since I became a parent, I have looked at shopping as much as a way to get out of the house as a way to get what I need. The mall offers food, movies, and an indoor playground, and you can often sit down and have a cappuccino (and a cookie or two) at the supermarket.

But like most other places families go, it has its hazards. Your child could get hurt in the shopping cart or on the escalator. He could get lost somewhere between "frozen foods" and "pet supplies." She could break one of those pricey vases (and cut herself) or swallow one of those nifty refrigerator magnets.

But fear not, a little advance planning can help you all survive—maybe even enjoy—your ventures into the consumer world.

Kids in tow

A problem that hits the minute your child can walk is how to keep them from wandering away from you in the store. This varies with the child. One child may be content to stroll along at your side, while another prefers hide-and-seek among the discount racks. Strollers, incidentally, are a great way to keep your child where you want him, as long as he is willing to go along for the ride.

Carriers work well for small children and short trips. Just plan well and make sure you are able to carry your baby and your packages at the same time. (See "Strollers/Carriages/Carriers.")

Leashes are another practical, if controversial, method of keeping track of an active child. I don't like the look of them myself, but am forced to admit that they are preferable to losing an active toddler in a busy crowd.

Shopping carts

In many stores, you can corral your child by riding him in a shopping cart. You'll now find them at hardware stores, the craft mart, and discount stores, in addition to the supermarket. They let you move through the aisles at adult speed, without worrying about junior ducking behind the cat-food display.

But this boon to parent-kind is not without its drawbacks. More than thirty-five thousand children a year get hurt falling out of shopping carts or tipping them over, making them the leading cause of emergency-room-treated head injuries to kids under five. While researchers from Children's Hospital Columbus, Ohio, called for a redesign of the carts after a 1996 study determined that the majority of the injuries are the result of carts tipping over, no redesign has yet been achieved.

In the meantime, since I don't see parents giving up this convenience, following a few safety rules will prevent shopping cart injuries:

- *Don't leave your child unsupervised in a shopping cart.* If this sounds like the most ridiculously unnecessary piece of advice you've ever heard, keep in mind that your child is just as unsupervised if you've walked to the end of the aisle to grab a box of cereal as if you've had to run back out to the car because you forgot your wallet. The Ohio study found that at least 80 percent of parents leave their child unsupervised at some point while they are shopping.
- *Don't rely on an older sibling to watch your baby* in the shopping cart. About 40 percent of the injuries to children younger than two in the Ohio study occurred when an older sibling tipped over the cart.
- *Ride your child only in the seat provided,* never in the bottom of the shopping cart. If the cart is equipped with seat belts, use them, but keep in mind that they won't prevent the cart from tipping over.
- *Never allow your child to stand up in a shopping cart.* (This will be easier if you are there to supervise.)

Smart shopping

In addition to knowing where your child is, you should always be aware of what items she can reach—whether from the end of her leash, the seat of her stroller or cart, or her perch on your back. Stores are not babyproof. Breakable items and choking hazards are everywhere, and it's up to you to keep your child in check. It should be a hard-and-fast rule that your child never touches anything in a store without asking you first.

If your child becomes lost

No matter what precautions you may have taken, it is extremely important for your children to know what they should do if they are separated from you in a mall or store. Teach them not to look around for you (except for a quick look around the immediate area), but to go directly to the checkout counter and tell a store employee they are lost. It will take some practice before very young children can reliably identify store employees.

The child should give her full name and the name of the parent or adult who was with her. For smaller kids, I recommend that you slip a card or piece of paper with this information into their pocket. Children often clam up when they are scared, and having this information written down means the adults who need it can get it right away.

I also think it doesn't hurt for parents and children to carry each other's pictures. This way store security can begin an immediate search and have an idea of who they are looking for—parent or child. Small plastic key chains that hold a photo are a good way to get your child to carry both the photo and the information. They're good for parents, too.

Escalators

One convenience most tired parents are happy to find is the escalator. "Do we get to ride on the escalator?" is always my daughter's first question when we enter the mall.

I'm a little nervous around them, but as Lauren fearlessly charges ahead I've gotten a lot of practice on the moving stairs in recent years. My husband laughs about my six-year-old "helping

Mommy on the escalator," but the CPSC reports that escalators caused 7,300 hospital-treated injuries in 1994 alone.

- Watch out for untied shoelaces, drawstrings, scarves, or other loose clothing that could get caught in the escalator.
- Always hold your child's hands on the escalator, and don't let them sit or play on the steps. (If you're too loaded down with packages to hold hands, it's time to look for the elevator.)
- Don't take strollers, walkers, or carts onto the escalator. If these items get caught in the machinery, both you and your child could get hurt before the escalator is stopped.
- Face forward and hold the handrail, and make sure your child does the same.
- Don't stand on the edges of the steps, which could grab hold of your shoes and trip you.

Indoor playgrounds

The second place my daughter wants to head, immediately after she gets off the escalator, is the mall's indoor playground. And that's okay with me, since it helps her blow off some steam and gives me a chance to sit down and plan my strategy (and put my feet up).

Indoor playgrounds in general were judged a safe alternative to traditional outdoor playgrounds by the Consumer Product Safety Commission in 1996. Just remember to supervise your child properly, and these playgrounds can make your shopping trip a much more pleasant experience for you and the kids. (See "Playgrounds.")

Stress and the smart shopper

Of course, all of these safety rules will be easier to follow if you are taking your time. A relaxed, well-planned shopping trip is always safer (and more pleasant) than a mad dash, so the National Safety Council recommends planning a reasonable number of errands per trip and allowing plenty of time to get everything done. Dr. Christine Wood, of Failure Analysis Associates, has some additional suggestions:

- Go after naptime, when the kids won't be tired and whining.
- Feed the kids before going shopping so they won't nag you for food.
- Go when the stores are least crowded (early in the morning, during the week).
- Engage the child in the task. "Keep them busy and part of the activity with you," says Wood. "Just remember that this takes more time."

Resources

"Shopping Cart Dangers," *Pediatrics for Parents*, volume 16, number 5.
"Doctors Demand Better Shopping Carts" *Pediatrics*, February 1996.
"Falls from Shopping Carts Cause Head Injuries to Children" and "U.S. Consumer Product Safety Commission Escalator Safety Alert," from the Consumer Product Safety Commission; (800) 638-2772.
"Child Protection," from the National Center for Missing and Exploited Children homepage; http://www.missingkids.org.

SMOG

Smog, or dirty air, is an almost invisible hazard that can clearly damage your child's health. While air pollution is harmful to everyone, children, who spend more time outdoors and use more oxygen per pound of body weight than adults, are the ones most at risk. Their developing lungs and immune systems make them especially vulnerable to toxins present in the air.

And we're not just talking about inner-city kids. Even in rural areas, things like crop fires, pesticides, and dust from plowing fields can compromise the quality of the air. Children all over the country are exposed to the effects of bad air, and the American Lung Association estimates that more than half of America's kids are living in areas where smog is a pervasive problem, according to a 1995 report called "Danger Zones: Ozone Air Pollution and Our Children."

Something in the air

Smog itself differs from place to place and day to day. It is a kind of floating toxic soup made of several potential components:

- *Particulate matter* includes dust, dirt, smoke, or droplets small enough to breathe. This type of pollution comes from manufacturing, traffic, fires (including burning firewood), and many other sources. It is a problem in most Western states and the industrial cities on the Great Lakes. Studies published in the *American Review of Respiratory Disease* showed that children exposed to particulate pollution experience more than three times the amount of coughing, more than twice the amount of bronchitis, almost twice the normal amount of earache, and double the rate of asthma symptoms. A 1991 German study showed a 27 percent increase in the amount of croup among children exposed to particulate matter. This type of pollution is also suspected of increasing the development of cancer.
- *Sulfur dioxide,* produced from the burning of coal and oil in electric power plants and in paper mills, is usually a problem in rural areas where these plants are located. This includes parts of Arizona, Utah, and Montana, and the area east of the Mississippi River and north of the Ohio River. This pollutant causes tighten-

ing of the chest in healthy people, but only when they are exposed to very high levels. People with asthma, however, can experience severe reactions even at low levels.

- *Nitrogen dioxide,* a yellowish-brown gas produced mostly by car and jet engines, can be found in most urban air. The country's highest levels, however, are in the Los Angeles metropolitan area. Nitrogen-dioxide exposure is linked with an almost 30 percent increase in coughing, wheezing, and bronchitis in children, according to a study in the *American Journal of Epidemiology*. It also helps create ground-level ozone.

- *Ozone at the ground level* (not to be confused with the protective layer in the earth's atmosphere) is created when noxious chemicals in the air react with sunlight, and is a major health risk in most urban areas. The compounds that create ozone come from the burning of gasoline and other fuels, paint, solvents, and chemical manufacturing. Ozone exposure is highest in Los Angeles, Houston, Chicago, and the coastal metropolitan area from Virginia to Maine, but most EPA urban-air testing stations register excessively high levels at least several days a year. Ozone causes eye irritation, chest pains, shortness of breath, and coughing.

- Carbon monoxide is a colorless, odorless gas produced by the incomplete burning of fuels. Two thirds of CO emissions in the United States come from cars, trucks, buses, etc. The major metropolitan areas on both coasts, as well as Spokane, Las Vegas, Denver, and Salt Lake City, are the areas of highest exposure. Breathing carbon monoxide reduces the blood's ability to transport oxygen, causing severe health effects at high levels. (See "Carbon Monoxide.")

Breathing easier

Unfortunately, toxins in the air can't just be cleared away the way you would clear dust and dirt out of your house. This makes avoidance your best strategy, so find out what's dirtying up your air and watch for reports that pollution levels are high.

Most major newspapers and weather reports in areas where air pollution is a problem list what is called the Pollutant Standards Index. The PSI predicts the levels of four common pollutants for the next day: ozone (the main ingredient in urban smog), carbon monoxide, nitrogen dioxide, and PM10 (particulate matter less than 10 microns wide). The scale ranges from 0 to 500, with a score of 100 or more indicating unhealthy air conditions. If you can't find a report in your newspaper or on your local TV weather forecast, you can call your local air-quality management district to find out whether pollutant levels will be high.

A bad air day

When pollution levels are above one hundred, it is best to stay indoors as much as possible. Ozone dissipates when it comes into contact with household surfaces, and if you are somewhere with a central air-conditioning or heating system, you can use it to help filter out particulate matter. If you do have to go outdoors, it is best to avoid strenuous exercise. This means your child's school should schedule outdoor physical activities to avoid peak smog hours.

You should be extra cautious if you live in a high-risk area, such as near heavy industry, fields that are being burned or plowed, or freeway on-/off-ramps. Urban residents should beware high-risk weather conditions, such as a hot, sunny day. Ozone, which is usually the largest component of urban air pollution, is created by sunlight, and levels are highest from late morning until after sunset, when the ozone in the air has dissipated.

Resources

"Air Pollution," from the National Heart, Lung, and Blood Institute Information Center; (301) 251-1222.
"Smog and Your Family's Health: Recognizing Symptoms, Understanding

Smog Reports, Avoiding Exposure to Dirty Air" and "Air Pollution Episodes: When to Blow the Whistle on Outdoor Activity," from the South Coast Air Quality Management District; (909) 396-3456.

SPORTS

I've heard many a health expert say that sports are an essential for kids, and with the obesity rate among kids under twelve up 25 percent in the past decade, who could call them wrong. If your daughter or son would rather spend time on the field, track, or court than in front of the tube, do all you can to encourage them.

Just keep in mind that all sports have risks along with their benefits. The U.S. Consumer Product Safety Commission reports that four million children a year are treated in emergency rooms for sports injuries, and another eight million are treated by their pediatrician.

This makes it important for players and their parents to know what they are getting themselves into well before the season begins. Knowing the risks involved with the sport your child chooses will go a long way toward preventing injuries.

Team players

Before your child tries out for a sport or joins a team, it's a good idea to get in touch with the coach. Get her or his take on the physical demands of the sport and of the team. What type of physical conditioning will be required, and what type of shape will your child need to be in to play? Making sure your child is in top condition before participating can reduce the risk of injury during the season.

Another important thing to find out is whether players in the league are grouped by age, or by size and ability. Children grow at very different rates, and if players are grouped solely by age, your seven-year-old could end up playing against children much bigger, stronger, and more skilled. This could lead to a disappointing season and, much worse, expose your child to greater risk of injury.

If the league doesn't group by size and your child is small for his age, consider signing him up for a team with kids a year younger, or switching to a noncontact sport.

You should also know what type of safety equipment will be provided for your child and what items you may need to buy. This may require a little homework on your part. Some safety equipment that has been proven to greatly reduce injury risk is not commonly required by sports teams. Any equipment your child uses should be nationally approved by either the National Operating Committee on Standards for Athletic Equipment (P.O. Box 20626, Kansas City, MO 64195) or the American National Standards Institute (1430 Broadway, NY, NY 10018).

If the equipment is provided by the team, make sure they have equipment that fits your child properly and is in good condition. Using worn or poor-fitting equipment can cause injuries. This is also true of shoes. Make sure your child's shoes are in good condition, fit well, and are appropriate for the sport. If you have trouble navigating the athletic-shoe aisles, ask the coach what to buy.

Inspect the courts, tracks, or fields your child is playing on to make sure they are in good condition. They should be free of potholes or debris, and generally well maintained.

Choosing a good coach

Certification of some sort helps ensure that your child's coach at least has some basic knowledge of injury prevention, conditioning, and psychology of the sport. But twelve states—Hawaii, Indiana, Maine, Massachusetts, Michigan, New Hampshire, North Dakota, Ohio, Oregon, Pennsylvania, Rhode Island, and Vermont—do not require any sort of teaching or coaching certificate for interscholastic sports.

This means that anyone could be hired to fill these positions, and your child could fall into the hands of someone who has no sports safety training. In fact, the National Youth Sports Safety Foundation estimates that 90 percent of the coaches in the United States have never taken classes to learn about the sport they are coaching.

No matter what state you are in, you should thoroughly check any potential coach's credentials, and talk to them about their conditioning plan. Get a copy in writing, if possible, and run it by your pediatrician.

You should also make sure your child's coach has a good emergency plan in place for dealing with serious injuries, and first-aid supplies readily available. Someone certified in first aid and CPR should always be there when the team practices or plays a game. The coach should have an assistant who can call for help or stay with the injured athlete while she does so. She should know how an ambulance would access the playing field, have transportation on hand if a player's injury is not serious enough to require an ambulance, and have emergency phone numbers for the parents/guardians or all athletes.

Getting physical

Before your child begins participation in any sport, she should have a thorough preseason history and medical evaluation, according to the American Medical Association Committee on Medical Aspects of Sports. These checkups help determine his fitness for the sport and detect any conditions that might cause injury during play. Even kids as young as six to ten need preseason physicals, says the National Youth Sports Safety Foundation—whether your league requires it or not.

The preseason exam is best performed by your athlete's pediatrician or family doctor, who has easy access to the child's medical history. But a routine physical examination isn't enough to determine whether your child is ready for her sport. The exam must include height, weight, vital signs, vision and dental screening, and a physical exam that tests flexibility, body composition, strength, speed, agility, power, balance, and endurance. Another important part of the exam is a review of the child's medical history, which can help identify more than 70 percent of all medical problems.

The ideal time for this exam is at least six weeks before the season starts, and before training and practice begin. This way any medical problems found can be corrected or rehabilitated before the season begins, and your child won't miss out.

Helmets

There are helmets for almost every sport these days, and with good reason. The National Youth Sports Safety Foundation considers helmets one of the most important pieces of safety equipment because they help protect against brain injuries, the leading killer and cause of disability in children and young adults. About 10 percent of all traumatic brain injuries are caused by sports, so take your child's helmet seriously.

Your child will need a helmet designed for the sport she will play, because different sports have different types of risks. But there are some quality standards that apply to all helmets. Helmets should fit snugly, with only one or two inches between the eyebrows and the ridge of the helmet. Chin straps should be kept tight and centered, and if there is a face guard, it should not move when the helmet is in place.

Beware helmets that have been passed down in a family or used for many years by a team. They may be soft, cracked, or have stretched insets that keep them from fitting correctly. These helmets don't offer the protection your child needs. Also beware any hel-

met that has survived a fall. It should be checked for cracks and replaced if necessary.

In many cases, your child's coach will take responsibility for
making sure helmets fit well and are in good condition. But you are
the parent, and the responsibility for your child's safety is ulti-
mately yours. The Sporting Goods Manufacturers Association
([407] 842-4100) can give you more information on helmets and
standards.

Mouth guards

Children lose teeth. But if they're participating in sports, they could
lose them when they shouldn't. Wearing a mouth guard—especially for sports like basketball, hockey, football, gymnastics, skate-
boarding, soccer or volleyball—can lessen the chances of this
happening by as much as 60 percent.

Mouthguards also cushion blows that might otherwise cause
concussions or broken jaws. But not all offer the same protection.
Stock mouth guards, purchased at a sporting-goods store and not
fitted to the individual in any way, offer the least protection. Mouth-
formed protectors, which are fitted at home, and custom-made
mouth guards offer greater protection. They are available at a range
of prices, and differ in comfort and fit.

Quality guidelines for mouth protectors are available from the
American Society for Testing Materials at (215) 299-5400.

The eyes need it

Virtually all young athletes need to use protective eyewear during
sports play, according to the American Academy of Ophthalmology and the American Academy of Pediatrics. And John B. Jeffers,
M.D., who chairs the Eye Safety and Sports Ophthalmology Committee for the American Academy of Ophthalmology, says kids

should start protecting their eyes as soon as they start playing sports.

Jeffers recommends using only goggles purchased from an optician, who can ensure that they fit properly. The goggles should have a polycarbonate lens and a frame with a molded temple. They are safer than goggles with hinges, which tend to be weak.

Getting your child to wear the goggles may be difficult, since most professional athletes don't use them and most leagues don't require them. But goggles could have prevented almost seventeen thousand serious eye injuries to kids under fourteen in 1993, and they could save your child's sight.

Warming up

Your young athlete may want to be a hot player, but if she isn't warmed up first, she may spend more time on the injured list than on the field.

"I think many people have the misconception that warming up and stretching are the same thing," says Head Athletic Trainer Ned Bergert of the California Angels, who compares a muscle to a lump of clay. "If you take a lump of Play-Doh and try to stretch it, it will just crumble," he explains. "But if you hold it and rub it and warm it up, then it will stretch and you can make it into anything you want."

To prevent injuries, kids should jog, run in place, do jumping jacks, jump rope, or engage in some other activity that raises your body's core temperature and creates a little perspiration.

Bergert recommends following this up with a round of slow-and-easy static stretching of the calves, hamstrings, quadriceps, groin, shoulders, forearms, trunk, lower back, sides, and stomach. Stretch in each position until there is a slight tension, but no pain, hold for twenty seconds, and repeat once.

The younger your child, the more flexible he will likely be. But

Bergert says proper warm-up and stretching is important for even the tiniest T-ball player because it helps develop good habits.

Water, water everywhere

Dehydration can make your child feel tired, dizzy, and weak, and keep her from playing her best. In hot weather, it can also leave her vulnerable to heatstroke or heat exhaustion.

And you can't rely on thirst to prevent it. Make sure your child drinks water before, during, and after practice and games. Water is the beverage of choice for keeping kids well hydrated. If it isn't provided by the team, make sure she has her own ample supply.

No pain

Once the season starts, about 20 percent of children injured during sports play will return to play too soon and be reinjured. Watch out for win-at-all-costs attitudes in yourself, your child's coach, and other players. If winning is that important, your child may feel she has no choice but to play while injured or in pain, especially if she is a "star" member of the team. Playing while injured can result in permanent injury or disability.

Kids who have a serious sprain with swelling or bruising, torn ligaments, numbness, trouble breathing, abdominal pain, or head injuries should not be allowed to continue playing until they are examined by a doctor, according to Dr. David Janda, director of the Institute for Preventative Sports Medicine in Michigan.

Baseball/softball

Baseball is one of America's favorite sports, and it—not football or hockey—causes the greatest number of sports-related deaths in children ages five to fourteen, according to the Consumer Product Safety Commission. It is also the cause of hundreds of thousands of injuries.

Sliding accounts for three fourths of all baseball and softball injuries (and led to thirteen thousand emergency-room visits in 1995). These injuries usually happen when the player's foot or leg collides with a base that is anchored to the ground. Leagues should use bases that break away when the player hits them to prevent these types of injuries, says Dr. David Janda, of the Institute for Preventative Sports Medicine. The breakaway base is anchored to the ground only with suction cups, which release on impact and spare the players' feet ankles and legs.

Janda found that such bases reduced injuries by 96 percent. The Consumer Product Safety Commission recommended in 1996 that youth baseball leagues start using breakaway bases, but didn't make their use mandatory. If your child's league doesn't use them and won't consider installing them (they are expensive), your child's best protection is to learn to slide safely. Moby Benedict, former head baseball coach for the University of Michigan, recommends a bent-leg slide, with the front leg bent and the other straight. Sliding headfirst is dangerous, because players might get stepped on.

Another major cause of injuries, and the cause of almost all baseball deaths, is being hit by the ball—either in the head or the chest. A ball leaves the average Little League pitcher's hand at about 60 mph, and line drives are routinely hit back at that same pitcher at speeds of 90 mph. A blow to the head can cause fatal brain damage, while one to the chest can cause arrhythmia, short-circuiting the heart. About sixty children have been killed this way in the last ten years, says the CPSC.

Your child can protect her head by wearing a batting helmet both in the batter's box and while running the bases. The team should have batting helmets of several sizes so that your child can find one that fits snugly. The helmet should be securely strapped on whenever it is worn and fitted with a protective face guard.

To protect the chest, the only real solution at this point is for players to learn how to get out of the way of a bad pitch. Most kids turn in to the baseball and get hit in the chest, which could stop the heart and prove fatal. What they should do is turn away from the ball so they get hit in the back. It will still sting, but the heart is safe.

Other attempts to reduce the number of deaths from blows to the chest, such as the use of softer balls and chest protectors, have proven controversial. Softer balls can decrease the damage from a blow to the head, but Janda's studies have shown that they can worsen the impact to the chest. The softer balls are heavier than regular balls, and hit a player's chest with more force. In fact, Janda reports that the only youth baseball player killed in 1995 was hit by a softer ball. Chest protectors, according to Janda's research, spread out the ball's impact and actually transfer more of its energy to the heart than the ball would alone.

Another common type of injury in baseball is an overuse injury best known as "Little League elbow." This condition is the direct result of allowing a child to overtrain or to pitch too many innings in a row. The best treatment is prevention, and your child's coach should set and enforce strict limits on how much players are allowed to pitch.

It is recommended that children under age eight not pitch. They are too young to learn how, and throwing wild pitches can injure their elbows and any batter who gets in the way.

Basketball

Basketball is responsible for more than 221,000 injuries to children per year, with more than 75 percent of these taking place during informal, unorganized games.

To prevent injuries, players should wear properly fitted shoes with nonskid soles and knee and elbow pads. Goals and the walls behind them should be padded. Younger players should use lighter-weight foam or rubber balls instead of the regulation leather balls. Since these conditions are less likely to exist in unorganized games, where most injuries occur, it pays to check out any court your child is using.

There's another danger to kids who love basketball that probably wouldn't cross most parents' minds. The scenario goes something like this: An undersized devotee of the sport tries to emulate his slam-dunking hero by using a springboard, stepladder, etc. to launch himself toward the hoop. As he flies forward, ball in hand, mouth wide open in an inspired holler, his teeth get tangled in the net and yanked out of his mouth. So keep an eye on that driveway hoop, and keep tempting objects like trampolines well clear of the net.

Field hockey

This sport has been gaining popularity over the past two or three years, probably because it is easy to learn and requires little equipment. But to prevent common injuries such as bruises, ankle sprains, and stick injuries to the face, hockey players should wear mouth guards, eye guards, and shin guards. If the game is on Astro-Turf, special turf shoes will help prevent foot and ankle injuries.

Football

Tackle football is a high-contact, collision sport not recommended for children under age twelve. Close to 190,000 children ages five to fourteen were injured playing football in 1994, according to the CPSC.

If your older child is playing football, make sure he wears shoulder, hip, tail, and knee pads and thigh guards. His helmet should fit properly, and be reconditioned, retested, and re-certified every year. But it's also worth checking to see how *old* the team's helmets are. The National Youth Sports Safety Foundation recommends that all youth football helmets be retired after eight years of use. A broken air cell inside a football helmet means it won't fit properly and offers inadequate protection.

But no helmet can completely protect against head injuries.

Janda recommends that parents take concussions in their football-playing children very seriously, and believes kids should stop playing for good if they've suffered three concussions.

Your child's league should teach proper techniques such as keeping the head upright when being tackled or tackling. Dangerous practices like spearing, butting, ramming, clipping, or blocking below the waist should be strictly forbidden.

Gymnastics

Common injuries from this popular sport involve traumatic injuries from falls and dismounts, overuse injuries such as sprains and strains, fractures, dislocations, and back problems.

Gymnasts should never practice alone and should always have qualified spotters with them to help prevent injuries from slips and falls. Equipment should be properly maintained and set up, with sufficient mats. Gymnasts should dress in clothing that lets them move freely, but doesn't get in the way of a safe performance. Coaches should also make sure that the training fits the child's age and ability level. Gymnasts should never be pushed into trying something they aren't prepared for.

Ice hockey

You've probably watched professional hockey players slamming each other into the boards on TV, and the thought of your five-year-old out there on the ice might make you cringe. But the little guys aren't usually the ones who get hurt. Five-year-old hockey players can't get up the speed and don't yet have the weight to deliver a bone-crushing check or a nose-smashing slapshot. It's when they get older, faster, and heavier that you need to worry.

But no matter what your child's age, outfitting with the right safety equipment is essential. Players should wear helmets with face mask, and shoulder, shin, elbow, hip, and tendon pads, padded hockey pants, gloves, and athletic supporters. It is also vital to buy your child a properly fitting pair of skates to prevent leg and ankle twists. Skates should fit tightly, with some movement in the toe but not the heel.

Skating/skateboards

In-line skates and skateboards cause more than 100,000 injuries a year, but protective equipment such as helmets, knee, elbow, and wrist guards can help prevent most of these.

A November 1996 study in the *New England Journal of Medicine* found that the typical skating injury is to a beginning skater who is not wearing safety equipment, and concluded that protective equipment could prevent more than a third of serious skating injuries.

Skaters should also keep to smooth, paved surfaces that are free of sand, water, gravel, or dirt, and should avoid skating at night when it is difficult to see obstacles that could cause a fall.

Soccer

This sport is popular with children as young as three, and about five million kids now play soccer.

The riskiest part of the sport is heading the ball, or using the head to deflect the ball during play. It has been shown to cause concussions, neurological problems, and maybe even eventual permanent damage to the brain. Kids under age nine shouldn't be heading the ball under any circumstance, in practices or games, says Dr. David Janda of the Institute for Preventative Sports Medicine. And heading drills shouldn't be overdone.

When learning the technique, kids under age eleven should use a smaller, lighter ball. And David Simeone, a coach with U.S. Soccer, recommends letting some air out of the ball at first and not letting players head kicked balls when they are learning. For drills, the ball should be thrown to them underhand. Kids should also learn the right way to head the ball—with the chin tucked to stabilize the head and neck, impacting the ball at the hairline, slightly above the forehead, where the skull is thickest.

Another big risk in soccer is from movable soccer goals, which can tip over and kill children who climb on them, or even be blown over on children by the wind, as happened in a 1995 Michigan case. To prevent this, goals should be securely anchored or counterweighted. Players are also injured or even killed when they collide with the goalpost, which should be padded to prevent serious damage.

Soccer players should be protected with shin guards, and should wear shoes with molded cleats or ribbed soles to provide adequate traction. It pays to spend a bit more for safety equipment. Janda found that more expensive shin guards using an air padding system provided 30 to 35 percent better protection.

Winter sports

Almost ninety thousand children were injured while enjoying winter sports in 1994, according to the Nemours Foundation at the Du Pont Hospital for Children. Two things all snowbunnies need to watch out for are their eyes (so wear protective goggles to keep them safe from protruding branches, etc.) and the sun. Harmful UV rays are less filtered at high altitudes, and reflect off white snow and ice. (See "Sun.")

Another big winter-sport hazard kids face is having to use equipment that is too big for them. Getting hand-me-down boots, skis, or snowboards from older siblings may save parents money, but this ill-fitting equipment may cost their younger child a painful or life-threatening injury.

Boots that are too big put extra stress on a child's foot and ankle. Skis or snowboards that are too big are difficult for a child to control. So get stuff that fits.

Kids also need safety equipment for many winter sports. Snowboarding and ice skating require helmets and knee, elbow, and wrist pads, just like in-line skating. And snowboarders—especially those just learning—may want to invest in some extra padding for body parts likely to get a whacking.

But the better part of injury prevention is learning to ski, snowboard, skate, or sled safely.

Kids who are sledding should find a hill that is free of obstacles (trees, rocks, poles) and not too steep. The bottom of the hill should also be clear of hazards, since sleds are tough to steer. Children should sled only on packed snow—not ice—and ride sitting up. It isn't safe to crowd too many people onto one sled, and of course kids shouldn't ride a sled being pulled by a car or snowmobile.

Skiers, skaters, and snowboarders should use the proper trails or areas, and avoid hotdogging or taking on a trail that's beyond their ability.

One winter sport that should be completely off limits to kids under sixteen, according to the American Academy of Pediatrics, is snowmobiling. Some models can travel at more than 100 mph, and weigh four hundred to six hundred pounds. That's just too much for a kid to handle.

No matter what sports your child chooses, the bottom line is to have fun. And if she stays safe and injury-free, she'll be free to enjoy herself and play her best.

Resources _____

"Sports Your Child Shouldn't Play," by Susan Gilbert, *Redbook,* April 1996.

"Study of Protective Equipment for Baseball," "Safety Commission Warns About Hazards with In-line Roller Skates," and "CPSC to In-line Skaters: Skate but Skate Safely," from the Consumer Product Safety Commission.

"Body Language," by Art Carey, *Philadelphia Inquirer,* May 30, 1994, January 23, 1995, and October 2, 1995.

"Dehydration Dos and Don'ts," *Pediatrics for Parents,* volume 16, number 7.

Dr. Gerard Varlotta, clinical assistant professor of rehabilitation medicine,

New York University School of Medicine and team physician for the New Jersey Rockin' Rollers professional roller hockey team.

"Play It Safe," from the American Academy of Orthopedic Surgeons; (800) 824-BONES.

"Health Notes," by Lidia Wasowicz, for UPI, October 1, 1996.

"Winter Sports: Have Fun, Be Safe," from the Kids Health Organization Web site of the Nemours Foundation; http://www.kidshealth.org.

"Keeping Soccer Safe," by Tracey Feeney, *Advance for Physical Therapists,* August 14, 1995.

"Padded Goalposts Take Kick at Serious Injuries," by Jeff Brooke, *The Medical Post,* February 14, 1995.

"Heading for Trouble?", *Sports Illustrated for Kids,* May 1996.

"Safe at Any Base," by Patricia Ansett, *Detroit Free Press,* February 22, 1993.

"Softer Baseballs and Padded Vests Are No Safeguards," *The Miami Herald,* March 15, 1992.

"Little League Safety Is Hot Topic of Debate," by Jim Cnockaert, *The Ann Arbor News,* June 6, 1996.

Fact sheets on preparticipation physical exams, football injuries, soccer injuries, baseball injuries, helmets, dental injuries, fall-sports safety, sports and injuries, and tips for athletes, from the National Youth Sports Safety Foundation; (617) 449-2499.

STAIRS

Falls down stairs injure millions of children a year, and the stairs your child is most likely to be going up and down are the ones right there at home.

Falling down

Stairs are especially dangerous to babies who can't yet walk (or walk very well) and children who may not be paying attention to where they are going. To keep these children from taking a tumble, put baby gates (the kind with the pressure bar, not the accordion kind; see "Baby Gates") at the top and bottom of every staircase in your home.

If your little one is big enough to be on the stairs unassisted, some commonsense rules will keep the whole family safer:

- Your stairway should be well lit, with light switches at both the top and the bottom.
- No one in your family should set *anything* down on the stairs— even for a minute.
- Your stairway should always be in good repair. Be on the lookout for loose carpeting or loose or broken railings.
- No one should run up or down the stairs.

The next step

There is one other type of hazard associated with stairways: strangulation. If the railings on your stairs are spaced more than 2 3/8 to 3 inches apart, or if your stairs are the "open-back" type, your child's body could fit through while her head gets stuck.

If your railings are too far apart, you can either have Plexiglas installed or buy a simple sheet of tie-on netting to keep kids from slipping through. If you have open-backed stairs, you may have to call in a professional to handle the job.

Resources

"Falls" fact sheet, from the National Safe Kids Campaign.
"Preventing Kids' Falls Is a Matter of Physics," by Lawrence G. Proux, *The Washington Post*, January 31, 1995.

STRANGERS

Of all the things that can harm your child, the one most likely to give you nightmares is stranger abduction. And you don't have to look further than the headlines to see that it happens.

This is one hazard for which prevention is the *only* cure. And that means that you and your children have to stay on your toes and be aware of dangerous situations. Robin Webb, creator of a child safety program called KeyEye, says that the most important thing you can teach your child about staying safe is to follow their instincts.

"Nature has given us a thing we call intuition. We've got to learn to trust this feeling. If it doesn't feel right, don't do it," he says in his child safety video for kids. Learning to trust their judgment and picking up a few good safety habits can help keep your child out of harm's way.

Teach your children

- What to do if they get separated from you in a public place.

  They should not look for you. They should quickly and quietly go to the nearest store checkout counter, security office, or lost-and-found and tell the person in charge they are lost. When I explained all this to my daughter before a recent trip to the mall, she asked, "But what if I'm outside." This was a problem I hadn't considered and the literature didn't cover. We decided that she should go into the closest store and go up to the counter to tell them she was lost.
- Not to get into a car or go anywhere with anyone (even someone they know) unless you have said it is okay.

  Your child should not accept a ride from anyone, under any circumstances, without checking with you first.
- Not to open the door to anyone they do not know or aren't sure about.

- Not to let callers know they are home alone when they answer the phone.
- To call out, "Hi, Mom. I'm home!" when they are coming home alone.

  This will make anyone who might be stalking your child think there are adults waiting in the house.

- Not to go near anyone's car to talk to them, and to stay away from anyone following them—in a car or on foot.

  Keeping kids away from the car keeps them out of reach of the person inside.

- Not to try to help any grown-up who is asking them for help (for directions, to find a lost puppy, etc.).

  Kids need to understand that grown-ups shouldn't be asking for help from children. If your child thinks a person really needs help, they should go get another adult.

- Not to believe anyone who tells them their parents are in trouble and tries to get the child to go away with them.

  Remind them that you would only send someone they know to come and get them in an emergency.

- To scream, "Help! This is not my mother," or "This is not my father," if someone is trying to take them away.

  If a child simply screams and cries, witnesses might just think the child is having a tantrum, and fail to intervene.

- To use the "buddy system" and always go places with a friend, if possible.
- Not to leave their yard or play area, or go into someone else's home, without your permission.
- To call home when they have arrived at a friend's house for a visit.
- Not to hitchhike.
- Not to keep secrets for adults—especially secrets that make the child uncomfortable.

  Your children should know (and if they don't, you should tell them) that they can always tell you anything that is bothering them without fear of blame or punishment.

- That they can say no, loudly, to any adult who wants to touch them in a way that makes them feel uncomfortable or hurts them, take their picture, or take them somewhere they aren't supposed to go.

Mothers of prevention

Besides teaching your children what they should and shouldn't do to stay safe, there are a few things you can do to help them out. The first is to know your child. Know where she goes, who her friends are, and what is going on in her life. When he is not with you, know where he is. If there is a new person in his life, know who it is.

According to the National Center for Missing and Exploited Children, you should be especially alert to a teenager or adult who is paying an unusual amount of attention to, or spending an excessive amount of money on, your child. You should also watch for abrupt changes in your child's behavior, as that may be a signal that something is wrong.

You should carefully screen any adults who will be interacting with your child—babysitters, child-care workers, coaches, etc.

The one thing you should *not* do (and this may run contrary to what you have heard) is establish a "code word" so that your child won't go anywhere with a stranger. The presence of a code word gives a stranger your child should be running away from the chance to start a conversation and win the child's trust. It also lulls the child into a false sense of security, because they tend to forget about the possibility of a stranger who doesn't know the code word using force to take them away.

Resources

"Basic Rules of Safety for Children and What You Can Do to Prevent Child Abuse and Exploitation," from the National Center for Missing and Exploited Children; (703) 235-3900.

"Safety Tips," from the KeyEye Web site, <http://www.keyeye.com>, and the KeyEye child safety video; (800) 442-6322.

STREET SAFETY

Think back to the last time your child crossed a street. It probably wasn't very long ago. Was he with you or another adult? Did he cross alone? Did he cross carefully?

More than eight hundred children were hit and killed by cars or trucks in 1994, according to the National Highway Traffic Safety Administration, and if your child is of elementary-school age, she is at tremendous risk of becoming a pedestrian fatality.

Children this age cannot spot oncoming traffic as easily as an adult. Their field of vision is one-third narrower, says the Child Injury Prevention Program of the Utah Department of Health, and they have trouble figuring out which direction the sound of an oncoming car is coming from. Kids also find it tough to tell how far away a car is, or how fast it is going, and don't understand how much time and distance it takes for a vehicle to stop.

They tend to overestimate their ability to get out of a car's way in time and are easily distracted from the task of getting safely across the street. To top it off, kids are just plain hard to see, since they can be hidden by bushes, parked cars, etc.

Darting into the street causes 50 to 70 percent of pedestrian fatalities to kids under nine, so start your lessons in street safety by explaining to your young child that there are cars in the street, that he could get hurt, and that he must never go into the street without holding a grown-up's hand. But don't count on these words to keep your child safe. Children younger than nine should be closely supervised whenever they are near the street.

Crossing the road

However, your child can have her first lessons in crossing the street safely as soon as she is old enough to walk with you. But this means you have to be a good example. Never dart out from between parked cars, cross without looking, or cross against the light when you are with your child. Actions speak louder than words.

What you *can* do is make a game of crossing the street safely. Teach your child to pick the best place to cross. The corner is better than the middle of the street, a crosswalk is better, and a crosswalk with a traffic light is best. You should never choose to enter the street from between two parked cars.

Explain to your child the right way to cross, and then talk him through the crossing as you go:

- Stop at the edge of the street.
- Look left, right, and left again, and listen for oncoming cars before stepping off the curb. Ask your child what he sees in the street so you know that he is really looking for cars and not just turning his head.

  It is important to explain to your children that a green light at an intersection doesn't mean no cars will be coming. Children need to learn to watch for cars that may be turning right on the red light or may be still finishing a left turn when the light changes. They also need to understand that cars sometimes run lights illegally.

  Another thing you should explain to your child is that the lines on the crosswalk will not necessarily stop an oncoming car. Even in crosswalks, kids need to stop at the curb and look for traffic, because drivers may not see them.
- When there are no cars in the street, or all cars in the intersection have stopped and you are sure the drivers see you, walk (don't run!) across the street. Keep watching for cars all the way across.

Walking across driveways and alleyways is much like crossing a street, so you should teach your child that the same rules apply. Stop, look, and listen for cars, and go carefully across.

If you go through the whole process of crossing safely every time you take your child across the street with you, she should have it down cold by the time she is nine years old and able to start crossing by herself. Once she is crossing the street alone, you should take every opportunity to check up on her habits. When walking with her, let her take the lead and see if she crosses streets safely. When you see your child crossing a street alone (near your house, for example), watch to see that she does it correctly, and remind her of the need to cross safely.

Resources

"Preventing Pedestrian Accidents" and "Traffic Safety Outlook: Pedestrian Safety," from the National Highway Traffic Safety Administration.
"Is It Safe to Cross Now?", from the Utah Department of Public Health.

STROLLERS/CARRIAGES/CARRIERS

Stepping out with your baby is much easier thanks to the wide range of strollers, carriages, and different types of carriers available. Just remember that the world is not babyproof, and putting your child on your back or in a carriage doesn't mean you don't have to keep your eye on her. The added height and mobility will put your darling within reach of fascinating new ways to hurt himself.

Strollers and carriages

Accidents involving strollers and carriages, in fact, result in fifteen thousand emergency-room visits by kids under age five every year, according to the Consumer Product Safety Commission.

When buying a stroller, you should look for one that has a base wide enough to keep it from tipping over even if your child leans over the side (to get that toy she just dropped). The seat belt and crotch strap should be securely attached to the frame, and the buckle should be easy to use, since you have to use it *every time* you put your child in the stroller.

The leg openings should be small enough to keep your child from slipping out. If he slips feetfirst through a leg opening, his head could become trapped between the seat and the handrest bar and he could be strangled. If the stroller converts into a carriage, you should be able to close the leg openings when it is in the carriage position.

When you set the brakes, as you should whenever the stroller won't be moving, they should completely lock the wheels and hold firm.

If your stroller has a basket to hold life's necessities, it should be low on the back of the stroller and directly over or in front of the back wheels. This will prevent the stroller from tipping when you load it up. Don't hang purses or shopping bags over the stroller handle, or it might tip backward and land junior smack on his head.

When unfolding your stroller, make sure your child and her little fingers are well out of the way to keep them from getting pinched, or worse, amputated. And never use a pillow or extra mattress in a stroller or carriage, since the use of soft bedding for infants has been linked with risk of Sudden Infant Death Syndrome.

Carriers

If you need to get between the aisles of your favorite boutique, or go off-road, a carrier can be a great way to go. It makes you and baby a more compact package, and keeps baby secure and close to you.

If you decide to use a soft front carrier, it should be made of a durable (preferably washable) fabric, with sturdy adjustable straps. The carrier should be a good, snug fit that supports the baby's head, with leg openings small enough to keep the baby from slipping out, but large enough that they don't chafe his legs. The carrier should be checked occasionally for sharp edges, tears, or loose straps.

Once your baby is at least four or five months old and can support her own head, you may want to switch to a back carrier, which will make carrying her ever-increasing bulk a little easier on your back. In this case, you should make sure the carrier frame will not pinch the child where it folds up, and has padding over any metal parts that are near the baby's face.

The carrier should also have sturdy restraining straps to keep your child from standing up or trying to climb out of the carrier, and should be deep enough to support the baby's back.

Resources

Equipment Safety Checklist and *The Safe Nursery Buyer's Guide,* from the U.S. Consumer Product Safety Commission; (800) 638-2772.
"Safe and Sound for Baby," from the Juvenile Product Manufacturers Association, 2 Greentree Centre, Box 955, Marlton, NJ 08053.

SUN

Mr. Golden Sun just ain't what he used to be. Remember running outside to play on a sunny day as a child? Your mother probably never made you stop and put on sunscreen, and she may have even done a bit of basking herself. These days we know that putting on your sunscreen on a sunny day is as important as putting on your coat on a cold one.

The sun's UVA and UVB rays can cause burning, cell and tissue damage, premature wrinkling of the skin, and skin cancer, which is diagnosed in more than 700,000 Americans a year. Experts estimate that a person gets 50 percent of his lifetime sun exposure by age eighteen, and that too much exposure as a child and teenager is a major cause of skin cancer and premature skin aging.

In the dark

Of course, the simplest way to protect your kids from the harmful effects of the sun is to keep them out of it—at least during the hours when it is strongest. That means between ten A.M. and three P.M. When possible, schedule your child's outdoor activities to avoid those peak sun hours. If your child must be out in the sun during those hours (and kids often must be for school or sports activities, if not to keep them from hanging around the house and driving you crazy), be sure to take other measures to protect them.

These tips do not, however, apply to babies under the age of six months. An infant's developing skin and eyes are especially sensitive to sunlight and can be irritated by sunscreen. Keep babies this young out of the sun completely.

And don't forget that your kids are still being exposed to UV rays on cloudy or foggy days. In fact, the cool temperatures can fool you into thinking they're not getting burned, and it isn't until later that you notice the damage the clouds were hiding. UV exposure also increases with altitude, making sun protection an essential part of a trip to the mountains.

UV *what?*

The UV (ultraviolet) Index found in most major newspapers and weather reports can help you decide when to keep the kids in the shade. The scale from 0 to 15 predicts the risk of sunburn (due to the predicted intensity of UVB rays) for the following day at noon. Here's what the numbers mean, along with some recommendations from the Environmental Protection Agency and the Scripps Hospital SunSmart Program to help keep your family from getting burned:

0 to 2: Even the fair-skinned can handle a thirty-minute dose of the midday sun, but they should put on sunglasses to protect their eyes from its harmful rays.

3 to 4: Fair-skinned people can sun for just fifteen minutes, and even those who rarely burn should head in after an hour. Everyone out in this level of sun should put on sunglasses and sunscreen.

5 to 6 leaves just twelve minutes of sun exposure to the burn-prone, and fifty minutes for those with darker skin. Slip on some shades, slop on some sunscreen, and slap on a hat to protect your scalp and help shade your face.

7 to 9 signals burners to head indoors after a measly eight minutes. Sun warriors should join them after thirty-seven minutes. Even with your sunscreen, hat, and glasses, it's best to find shade.

10 or higher: Fair-skinned people beware, you can burn in just five minutes in a scorcher like this. Even the tan at heart will be overdone in just twenty-two minutes. If you must go out under these conditions, hat, glasses, sunscreen, and staying in the shade are a must. But your best bet is to stay indoors.

If you can't locate a UV report in your local paper or weather forecast, you can get one just about anytime by calling the U.S. Environmental Protection Agency Stratospheric Ozone Hotline at (800) 296-1996. Keep in mind, though, that the UV index predicts only the possibility of sunburn. But even if you are brown as a berry, the sun is damaging your skin, and you're exposed to increased risk of premature wrinkling and skin cancer. *Any* tan indicates skin damage.

Sunscreen

The heavy artillery in the war against sun damage is sunscreen. Since we live in the endless summer of Southern California, my six-year-old daughter wakes up every morning and puts on sunscreen before her clothes. And no matter what your climate, that's your best bet during the part of the year when the UV Index tends to be high.

Choose a sunscreen that's waterproof/sweatproof, with a Sun Protection Factor of at least 15, and apply at least thirty minutes before sun exposure to allow the skin time to absorb it. It should offer protection from both UVA and UVB rays. It's a good idea to try whatever brand you choose on a small area of your child's skin before an allover application. Some sunscreens contain fragrances or other ingredients that might cause an allergic reaction.

If there is a fragrance, make sure it's one your child enjoys. My daughter hated using fragrance-free sunscreen, but couldn't wait to put on the pineapple/coconut variety.

Whatever brand you choose, slop it on liberally. Depending on the size of your child, it could take a full ounce of protection for a full-body application. Don't forget details like the ears, back of the neck, and the part in the hair, and reapply every hour or two. Even waterproof products won't stand up to toweling off.

Clothing and hats

Clothes can be another important way to protect your child from the sun's harmful rays, but not just any fabric will do. A loose weave can let the sun shine in, and let your child burn right through what she is wearing. And in fact, a typical cotton T-shirt provides an SPF of only 5 to 9. So choose sun-wear that has a tight weave, preferably with long sleeves and long pants. (If your child won't stand for so much clothing on a hot day, remember that sunscreen.)

If you don't want to trust your child's skin to ordinary fabrics, there are a few manufacturers whose clothing is made specifically for its SPF protection. One of these is Sun Precautions' Solumbra line. The clothing, made of tightly woven cottonlike fabric providing an SPF factor of 30, comes in polo shirts, pants, and even long skirts, and includes a selection of hats—from wide-brimmed straw models to ultraprotective "legionnaire" designs for adults and children.

Hats are another important form of protection from the sun. They help shade the eyes and face and cover the scalp, which is usually left free of sunscreen. Some styles of hat, such as Solumbra's legionnaire, will even protect the back of the neck.

Sunglasses

I'm not just trying to be cool when I say that sunglasses are an essential. Exposure to the sun's ultraviolet rays has been linked to cataracts, skin cancer of the eyelids, and sunburn of the cornea— all conditions that can temporarily or permanently affect sight. These conditions can also build up over time, worsening with cumulative exposure to the sun and affecting children later in life.

But don't just go out and get your kid some cheap sunglasses. Take the time to find a pair that offers both UVA and UVB protection, since both types of rays can do damage. If your child wears prescription glasses, consider an investment in prescription sunglasses an investment in the health of your child's eyes.

The days of the healthy tan are over. And this generation of children will have to learn to give Mr. Golden Sun a little more respect. Keep your kids out of the sun when it's strongest, protect them with proper clothing, sunglasses, and sunscreen. They'll avoid painful sunburns and miss out on some of the long-term dangers that could strike long after they have children of their own.

Resources

"Sun & Sensibility: Burning Issues in Protection," by Rebecca Howard, *L.A. Parent* magazine, May 1996.

"Facts for Consumers: Protecting Kids from the Sun" and "Sunscreens," from the U.S. Federal Trade Commission; (202) 326-2222.

"Radiation Reminder," *Your Child's Wellness Newsletter,* November/December 1995.

Scripps Sunsmart UV Meter Reference Sheet, from Scripps Hospital, San Diego, CA; (619) 457-7238.

For information on Solumbra clothing, call (800) 882-7860.

SWIMMING/POOLS

Splashing, thrashing, screams for help. If this is your image of a child drowning in a pool, you haven't got the picture. Each year more than three hundred children ages four and under drown in swimming pools—without making a sound. Childhood drowning, experts agree, is a "silent event." Children under five don't understand the dangers of falling in the water, and just slip under without a sound.

And it happens fast. Once a young child falls into the water, he may swallow water, sink, and lose consciousness in less than a minute. After that, it only takes two or three minutes for the child to drown. This means that if you have a child—especially one under the age of five—near a body of water, your constant supervision is not enough to protect her.

Home sweet pool

Most children who drown are found in somebody's backyard pool—more than half of these in their own home. The majority of children, 46 percent, had last been seen in the house five minutes before they drowned, and in 70 percent of cases, one or both parents were around, according to the National Safe Kids Campaign. Almost all these children were not even expected to be in or near the pool at the time they were found in the water.

So if you have a pool and a child, creating layers of protection is your best defense against drowning. No barrier can keep children out of the pool completely, but by putting several obstacles in their path, you increase the time it takes them to get into the water and increase your chances of finding them before that happens. And since 33 percent of drownings happen at a friend's or relative's house, make sure anyone your child visits is following the same precautions.

Your child's first obstacle should be a five-foot-high fence or wall that surrounds the pool and separates it from the house. The wall or fence should have no foot- or hand-holds that help a child climb over it, which means chain-link fences should have diamond-shaped openings no larger than 1 3/4 inches. If the fence has bars or slats, they should be less than four inches apart to prevent a child from squeezing through.

All gates in this fence should be self-closing and self-latching, with the latch out of the child's reach.

You'll also have to take extra care to keep patio furniture, large toys, and anything else your child could use to scale your barrier away from the fence. Don't forget that a resourceful child bent on climbing could drag a chair or table across the yard.

If you can't put a fence between the pool and the house, all doors leading to the pool should be alarmed to alert parents when they are unexpectedly opened. It is best to choose a model that has a switch or keypad out of reach of children that lets an adult temporarily turn off the alarm for a single opening of the door. This way, you won't accidentally leave the alarm turned off when you have to run outside to do something.

A good second layer of protection is a power safety cover over the pool or an alarm system in the pool, whenever it is not in use. The cover should be strong enough to hold the weight of two adults and a child. Any water that collects on the cover should be removed quickly, because a child could drown in just a few inches of water. Always take the cover completely off the pool before swimming, because someone could become trapped under the cover and drown.

You should have a clear view of the pool or the spa from the house so you can see immediately if a child has fallen into the water. It is also a good idea to paint or tile the bottom of the pool or spa in a light color so anyone in the water is easier to spot.

You should have a diving board in pools only where the water is at least eight feet deep, to prevent divers from hitting the bottom. Ladders and steps at either end of the pool should be made of nonslip material, and so should the deck area around the pool.

Keep lifesaving devices, such as a life preserver, tied to a rope, in the pool area, and do not take them down to use them for play. You should also have a telephone in the pool area for use in emergencies, with emergency telephone numbers clearly posted.

Pool rules

- Never use your pool or spa if any of the grate outlets is missing or broken. A child could get caught in the suction and be held underwater.
- Keep nonwater toys away from the pool, where they might distract a child into falling in the water.
- Keep the water level in the pool within three to four inches of the top, to make climbing out easier.
- Never allow glass in the pool or pool area—even for adults.
- Keep all pool chemicals and equipment locked up and out of reach.
- Small children can also drown in wading pools, so empty them when you aren't there to supervise.

Spas

Since they can drown in even small amounts of water, children under five are in as much danger from a spa as from a full-blown pool. This means they require the same safety precautions, including fencing and safety covers.

Children can also become caught or have their hair tangled in the drain holes in spas with only one outlet. A person blocking the drain outlet causes the suction to increase, and can be held underwater by the extra suction. New safety standards require that spas have at least two outlets, which decreases the suction and prevents people from being trapped.

- Make sure your spa has at least two drains.
- Check the drain covers regularly to make sure they are not broken or missing, and have a professional check your spa once a year to make sure it is in safe condition.
- Know how to turn off the pump in an emergency.
- Keep the spa temperature at or below 104 degrees Fahrenheit.

Lakes, rivers, oceans

All children boating, swimming, or playing in or near lakes, rivers, streams, etc., should wear a U.S. Coast Guard–approved personal flotation device at all times. Air-filled inner tubes, "water wings," or other toys are no substitute. Almost 75 percent of children under twelve who drown in boating-related accidents are not wearing a PFD, according to the National Safe Kids Campaign.

Older children who can swim should be taught to be careful of changing depth, temperature, currents, and concealed hazards in natural bodies of water. Don't let them swim in water where you are not completely sure of the depth, temperature, currents, and other hazards. This goes double for jumping or diving.

Swimming lessons

I believe swimming is a skill every person should learn. It's fun, a great form of exercise, and could save your child's life one day—but don't count on it. About 25 percent of children who drown have had swimming lessons, according to the California Department of Health Services. Children may forget their swim skills if they unexpectedly fall into the water or become overtired, or may not be strong enough swimmers to handle the current in a natural body of water.

Many professionals warn that parents should never consider a small child waterproof, no matter how much swim instruction or experience he or she has had. Swimming lessons are no excuse for dropping your guard or being lax in fencing your pool.

The American Academy of Pediatrics recommends that parents choose a swim instructor with plenty of training and experience. Swim lessons for infants should always be done on a one-on-one basis, and the instructor or parent should never totally submerge the child. Organized group instruction is okay for children age three and older, in small groups with plenty of supervision.

In the swim

No matter where you are swimming with your child, following some safety rules will help keep accidents from happening.

- Never take your eyes off a child who is in or near the water—not even for a second.
- Teach the kids that it is not safe to run, push, or shove near the water.
- Do not allow screaming or false cries for help in the water. Remember the boy who cried "wolf."
- No one of any age should swim without a "spotter."

- If you have a party or other social gathering near the water, designate someone to watch the children and swimmers at all times.
- Teach your child the quickest and easiest way to get out of the water.
- Everyone over fourteen should know CPR, which must be started within minutes to save a person's life. Almost all children who still need CPR when they get to the emergency room die.

Resources

"Spas, Hot Tubs, and Whirlpools" safety alert, *News Splash! for Safety: Drowning Prevention for Parents With Pools,* from the U.S. Consumer Product Safety Commission.

"Toddler Drownings—a Preventable Tragedy," from the California Department of Health Services.

A Guidebook for Preventing Childhood Drowning and *Is Your Pool or Spa Protected?,* from the Orange County Immersion Injury Prevention Project; (714) 834-5728.

"Drowning Prevention Tips," from the Alisa Ann Ruch Burn Foundation; (800) 242-BURN.

Frame the Photo, Fence the Pool!, Injury Prevention Network Newsletter, Spring 1994, from the Trauma Foundation, San Francisco General Hospital; (415) 821-8209.

"Drowning in Infants, Children and Adolescents," *Pediatrics,* volume 92, number 2, August 1993, pp. 292-294.

"Children Aren't Waterproof," from the National Pool and Spa Institute; (703) 838-0083.

"Drowning" fact sheet, from the National Safe Kids Campaign.

"Is Your Pool Safe?", from the San Gabriel Valley Drowning Prevention Task Force; (818) 814-8811.

TELEPHONE

If your child is three or older, he should know how to use the telephone to call for help. Most children love to use the telephone, and this is a skill that could save a life.

If you live in a 911 service area, teach your child to call 911 in the event of any emergency. If you don't live in a 911 service area, look up the numbers of your local ambulance, fire department, and police department and post them near every phone in the house. If your child is too young to read, tape small pictures of a fire engine, ambulance, and police car next to each number. Explain what the pictures mean and when to call each number.

Your child should also know her full name, address, and telephone number so she can give these to the dispatcher if necessary. Teach her to give this information slowly in a calm, clear voice, and then to tell the dispatcher the problem. Your child should stay on the line and answer all the dispatcher's questions as best she can until she is told to hang up.

Use a toy telephone and practice calling for help until you are comfortable that your child could do it even if he was frightened or upset.

Cordless and cellular phones

If you have a cordless telephone in your house, make sure your child either knows how to turn it off and on or knows that he should use a different phone in an emergency.

If you have a cellular telephone, be sure to teach your child to push the "send" button after dialing. On a cellular telephone, the first information the child should give is his location, because the dispatcher won't have access to the address. Then the child should give his name and stay on the line until he is told to hang up.

Screening calls

If your child is old enough to be home alone, teach her to use the answering machine to screen calls. That way she only has to pick up if the call is coming from you, or from someone else she knows.

If your child does happen to answer the phone and someone she doesn't know asks if her parents are home, teach her to say that you are in the shower and can't come to the phone. Under no circumstances should your child ever tell a caller she is home alone, or give her name or address to anyone over the phone.

Resources

"Helping Children Cope with Disaster," from the American Red Cross.
Home Organizer for Medical Emergencies, from the American College of Emergency Physicians.
The KeyEye child safety program.
The Comcast Cellular Kids Watch program.

TELEVISION

Television delivers the outside world direct to the average child for several hours a day, and though it isn't generally thought of as a *hazard,* the tube does pose some threats to your child's well-being.

The first is the threat associated with a sedentary lifestyle. On average, kids are fatter and get less exercise than they used to, and television is one reason why. A reported 36 percent of American schools do not require physical-education classes, 70 percent of American children cannot pass the President's Physical Fitness Test, and 40 percent of kids ages five to eight show at least one heart-disease risk factor (inactivity, obesity, elevated cholesterol, or high blood pressure), according to the United States Physical Education Association. The fact that you will never see a juvenile television program interrupted for a commercial on broccoli and carrot sticks only compounds the problem.

The other hazard of television is that it can expose an impressionable child to too much too soon—be it sex, violence, or disturbing content on the evening news. On some occasions, that content can translate into emotions the child doesn't know how to handle. And children trying to imitate the violence they see in kids' shows on TV can hurt themselves—and other children.

A number of tools are available to parents looking to shrink television's impact on their children's lives:

Limit channel and content access. The least complicated way to handle the TV dilemma is to limit your child's access to certain channels or programs. One way of doing that is simply to pay attention to what your child is watching. This works most of the time—especially if you limit TV viewing to certain times of the day when you know what programs are on. But what if you're not there?

Congress has mandated (and manufacturers are trying to perfect) a computer chip, called the v-chip, which will read information coded into a program on the same band that carries closed-captioned information. Programs are rated on a numerical scale and viewers with the chip installed in their sets can adjust them to read the coding and screen out certain levels of sexual and violent content.

But since the v-chip isn't yet available, and may not be especially practical (you have to fiddle with several small knobs on the back of your set every time you want to activate or adjust it), other products have tried to fill the gap. There are programmable remote-control devices available that limit your child's television access to kid-oriented channels and networks. One such device, called Kid Control, is available as either a purple dog ("channel rover") or a red dinosaur ("remote-a-saurus") and comes preprogrammed with selections like the Disney Channel and Nickelodeon. It retails for about thirty dollars. Call (303) 267-5500 for product information.

Teach your child to be a wise media consumer. Of course, devices like Kid Control only work in your own home. But what happens when your child is at a friend's house, or somewhere else where access is not restricted? Telling your child, "If you go to Jennifer's house, you can't watch TV" won't necessarily keep her away from the set.

But what if your child sat down in front of a friend's television, decided that the program on was trash, and suggested they do something else? What if your child responded to a commercial for Sugar Marshmallow Crunch with, "Why do I need *that*?" This is the principle behind the concept of media literacy—teaching children to be wise television consumers so they can monitor their *own* viewing, at least to some degree.

This is an ongoing process and does require a commitment from you to watch and talk about enough TV with your child to get your message across. You can start with the commercials, and a question as simple as, "What do you think they are trying to sell us?" Follow up by discussing the actual product and comparing it with the image of the product the ad is trying to project (e.g., Do you think eating that cereal will really make you a famous basketball star? Would My Size Barbie really make a good friend?). Discuss programs your child watches and encourage them to consider the quality of the show. Is the show interesting, or is it just the only thing on? Can we learn anything from this program, or is it just using up half an hour of our time? You can start this approach with any child old enough to be spending time in front of the set, and I have seen the results kick in as early as age four. Encourage older children to keep a TV journal to keep track of how much television they watch and the quality of the shows. (Note: Making TV more work might also make it less attractive.)

The Center for Media Literacy in Los Angeles offers a wealth of materials to help parents, schools, and other organizations teach concepts like challenging violence, analyzing advertising images, combating stereotypes, and detecting violence in the news. For their current catalog, call (800) 226-9494.

Use your VCR. But the most effective weapon against commercial television I have found—at least thus far—is an unusual one: our VCR. My daughter has been allowed some access to television since before she entered toddlerhood, but has almost never watched anything but children's videos and PBS. These are both commercial-free, so my daughter, now six years old, is not used to having her programming interrupted by any outside force (other than Mom and Dad).

We first discovered the result of this happy accident one Saturday evening when we all sat down to watch a Disney film being shown on commercial television. When the first commercial came on, my daughter began to howl. She thought someone had turned off her video! And to this day, Lauren won't watch a program with commercials. I don't know if this strategy will work on a child already accustomed to commercial interruptions, but a wide selection of quality videotapes at least provides an acceptable, commercial-free alternative to programming you'd rather turn off.

Resources

The Center for Media Literacy; (800) 226-9494.
"TV and Food," *Pediatrics for Parents,* volume 16, number 5.

TOYS

My daughter had exactly two items on her Christmas list, and one was a Cabbage Patch Snacktime Kids doll, known to her as "Baby

Chews." So, during a last-minute rush through a crowded toy store, I snatched up the doll in question and tossed it into my cart without a second glance. The doll was by Mattel, a well-respected maker of children's toys, and it was my little girl's heart's desire. Of course it was safe!

A week later my desk at work was stacked with reports that the masticating doll had chewed the hair of more than thirty children right up to the scalp. Even the most conscientious parent can unintentionally bring home a bad toy.

We buy more than 1.7 billion toys a year, according to the Toy Manufacturers of America, and every year kids are hurt and killed by their playthings. Failure Analysis Associates, a consulting firm that investigates product injuries and accidents, received reports of 165,000 toy-related injuries treated in emergency rooms in 1994. Half of these were to children younger than five.

A toy story

Choking is the major source of toy-related fatality, according to Dr. Christine Wood of Failure Analysis Associates. And latex balloons or pieces of balloons are the most common toy children choke to death on. These balloons, which are not subject to government small-parts regulations, have claimed victims as old as five, and result in six deaths a year, according to a University of Minnesota study reported in December 1995. The study found that 29 percent of nonfood-related chokings were caused by latex balloons. Mylar balloons are safer, says Wood.

Small balls (marbles, Super Balls, balls with jacks, game pieces) are other common hazards, causing 19 percent of fatal chokings in the Minnesota study.

A good rule of thumb to use is that any toy—or any detachable piece of a toy—that would fit through a toilet-paper tube is a choking hazard and should not be given to a child under three years old.

Batteries—the small part of the toy that's not included—are another major choking hazard, as well as a chemical-burn hazard if they are corroded or your child chews through the casing. If your child is using a battery-operated toy, watch what happens when the toy is dropped. Often the battery cover will come loose, spilling the batteries out within the child's grasp.

Batteries are also a danger if they are used incorrectly. Trying to recharge a nonrechargeable battery could cause it to overheat and rupture, leaking dangerous chemicals that will burn the skin on contact. The same could happen if you use alkaline and carbon-zinc batteries together in the same appliance, or if you mix old batteries with new ones. The biggest hazard to children, however, is likely the fact that batteries can overheat if they are placed in a toy backward (positive end where the negative end belongs), so make it a rule that only adults change the batteries in the children's toys.

Riding toys follow balloons and small parts as a leading cause of toy-related death. These are primarily tricycles, and the accident usually involves a collision with a motor vehicle or the child riding into a swimming pool. Riding toys also accounted for forty thousand injuries in 1994, or 24 percent of all toy-related injuries. These mostly included scrapes and lacerations, and did not involve cars or pools. (See also "Bicycles," which were not included in these statistics.)

Projectile and flying toys like slingshots, darts, toy guns (but not BB or pellet guns), toy boomerangs, etc. accounted for 10,700 injuries in 1994, reports Failure Analysis Associates. These toys often cause eye injuries, and their "ammunition" (arrows, darts, or plastic pellets) can pose a choking hazard, according to the American Academy of Pediatrics.

Noise made by cap guns and other toys is also a hazard, says the AAP. While CPSC regulations limit the decibel level of caps to no more than 158, the AAP cautions that decibel levels as low as 100 can damage a child's hearing. And cap guns are especially damaging if used withing twelve inches of a child's ear, or if used indoors. (See "Noise.")

Another danger associated with noisy cap guns is the caps themselves. They are filled with pyrotechnic material, and could be accidentally ignited by friction if kept in a child's pocket.

Electric plug-in toys and hobby kits could seriously injure your child—especially if they are misused, warns the American Academy of Pediatrics. Frayed cords can cause electrical burns and shocks. Chemistry sets and hobby kits (even approved models) may contain toxic substances that can cause fires, explosions, and poisonings. These toys may provide wonderful creative and educational experiences, but make them experiences you *share with your child*. And store the items safely out of reach when you aren't there to provide the necessary supervision. (See "Art Supplies.")

Choosing the right toy

To a certain extent, you can rely on governmental and industry regulations to make sure your child finds only the safest toys on her favorite aisle at Toys "R" Us. "The standards that exist do provide a certain amount of protection," says Wood, who adds that these regulations do not relieve parents of all toy-choosing responsibility. Toys must still be matched to their prospective pediatric owners, and there are still some toys imported from other countries that may not meet the U.S. standards, though the CPSC does try to keep these out.

Toys that do not meet government safety standards, or are found to be unsafe by their manufacturers or through consumer complaints, are generally recalled. To find out if a toy has been recalled, or to report a toy-related injury, call the Consumer Product Safety Commission at (800) 638-2772.

But even some toys that do meet federal standards may not be the safest choice for your child. "You have to know your child and your child's capabilities," says Wood, adding that you also have to pay attention to the label to find toys that are appropriate. Most toys are labeled according to safety and interest guidelines, with the age range for which the toy is intended. Wood echoes the American Academy of Pediatrics' caution that buying a toy too advanced, or even too simple, for a child could lead to misuse of the toy and opens up the possibility of injury.

Toys to avoid

The American Academy of Pediatrics cautions against purchasing toys with:

- parts that could pull/break off and fit in a child's mouth, nose, or ear
- exposed wires or parts that get hot
- lead paint
- toxic materials
- breakable parts
- sharp points or edges
- glass or brittle parts
- springs, gears, or hinged parts that could pinch or entrap a child's fingers
- toys that make loud or shrill noises, which could damage a child's hearing
- stuffed animals containing small beanlike pellets a child could swallow or choke on

Another group of "toys" parents might want to reconsider are BB and pellet guns, 80 percent of which have the capability to penetrate skin, soft tissue, and even bone, according to the CDC Office of Statistics and Programming. The CDC reports that these guns cause thirty thousand emergency-room-treated injuries every year. About 1,400 of these injuries are to the eyes of children and teenagers.

Supervision

No matter how safe the toy, you can never assume it will be used "only as directed," so a watchful eye is always required. That teddy bear with the twinkling eyes could kill a child who pulls out one of those eyes and chokes on it. The cord on that pull-along duckie could become wrapped around her neck. She could break that snow globe and cut herself on the sharp plastic. "I think almost any toy could be used unsafely if kids are not supervised," says Wood. "Even though these products are designed for kids to use, that doesn't mean they can use them without supervision."

Wood recommends that parents at least stay within earshot of their toy-occupied youngsters no matter what they are playing with, and make periodic personal appearances to encourage safety. Nursery monitors can be useful if you are trying to keep tabs on the kids from another room—even if the children are beyond nursery age.

And be sure you have read the instruction label on any toy your child owns. The label might contain important cautionary infor-mation, and you won't know when a toy is being misused unless you know how to use it.

Oh, brother

Many little brothers and sisters are hurt when "sharing" toys meant for older siblings. "Monitoring that is a tough task," says Wood, who recommends using storage bins so the toys can be put out of reach of younger siblings quickly and conveniently. You should also ex-plain to your older child why it is important to keep her toys picked up. "But you can't rely on them to follow through. Just because you've explained to your five-year-old, that doesn't mean he's going to put his little Legos away," cautions Wood.

Pick up your toys

The AAP recommends that *all* toys be stored when not in use. (See "Child's Bedroom" for toy-chest guidelines.) This helps keep them from being stepped on or tripped over and goes a long way toward keeping them in safe (unbroken) condition. Toys should *never* be stored in their original packaging if it contains staples that could cut little hands, or plastic wrap, which could suffocate your child.

It's also a good idea to hold periodic toy inspections to weed out or repair anything that's broken—splinters on wooden toys, loose facial features (eyes, noses, etc.) on dolls or stuffed animals, tears in stuffed animals, or rust on metal toys. If you're ever in doubt about your ability to fix the plaything in question, throw it away and repair your child's broken heart with a newer, safer toy. It's much cheaper than that trip to the emergency room when she swallows Pookie's shoebutton eye, and it could save your child's life.

(For additional age guidelines, see the "Childproofing Checklists" section.)

Resources

"For Kids' Sake," "Household Batteries Can Cause Chemical Burns," "Don't Let Children Put Caps for Toy Guns in Their Pockets," *Manufacturers' Abbreviated Guide for Age-Labeling Toys: Matching Toy Characteristics to Children's Ages, Guidelines for Relating Children's Ages to Toy Characteristics, and Which Toy for Which Child: A Consumer's Guide for Selecting Suitable Toys,* from the U.S. Consumer Product Safety Commission; (800) 638-2772.

"Toy Safety Guidelines for Parents," from the American Academy of Pediatrics.

"Choking Children," Associated Press news bulletin, December 12, 1995.

"Federal Agency Says BB, Pellet Guns Are Not Toys," Reuters World Report news bulletin, December 14, 1995.

VISITING

It can be fun to take your children to visit Grandma and Grandpa, or other relatives and friends. But if the kids are small, a little away-from-home babyproofing may be in order. The amount of work you need to do will vary depending on the length of your visit and the ages of your children.

If you're just staying an hour or two, and your child isn't likely to explore much, you may just have to pick up one or two breakables and make sure your child plays only in certain areas of the home. But if, for instance, Grandma and Grandpa watch the kids on week-days while you work, you'll need to take the same babyproofing measures you would take in your own home. These temporary measures are meant only for shorter visits, and most will also work in hotel rooms.

Making sure your child is safe doesn't have to mean rearranging someone's entire house, but you should do the following:

- Take a look around the house—at your child's level—and move any obvious hazards out of reach. These might include scissors, breakable vases, objects small enough for your toddler to choke on, etc.
- Look for exposed electrical outlets. If your stay is a short one, you can just keep your child out of that general area. If you're staying longer (an entire afternoon or overnight), cover the outlet with masking tape. That will slow your child down enough for you to catch up with him.
- Find out where cleaners and medications are kept. If your stay is short, keep your child out of the area. If you're staying longer, move the items out of your child's reach. Medication is a common haz-ard to watch for when visiting a grandparent's house. Older people are more likely to be taking prescription medicines, and they are more likely to leave them in plain sight so they remember to take

them. If Grandpa or Grandma is worried about forgetting to take medicine that is put away, I suggest taping a large, brightly colored reminder note where the medicine is usually kept.

- If your child is young enough that she puts things in her mouth, move all houseplants in the area where she will be playing out of reach.
- If your child is new to walking, or is still trying to learn, move unsteady pieces of furniture out of heavy traffic areas if you plan to stay awhile. If something with sharp corners, such as a glass-topped coffee table, can't be moved, it can be covered with a thick blanket to cushion the corners.
- If there are other children living in the house, be careful about letting your child play with their toys. Toys for older children may have small parts your child could swallow.
- If there are locking doors in the house, you can keep your child from locking himself in by covering the latch with masking tape.
- If you are staying overnight, bringing a night-light or two could keep your child from tripping and falling in the dark if she has to get up alone.

If you have an especially active toddler, and your visit is only going to last a couple of hours, it probably won't be worthwhile to babyproof the whole house. Bringing a portable play yard or playpen, or a couple of baby gates, will keep your child confined to a smaller area of the house. This way you can concentrate on babyproofing only one room, and then relax and enjoy the visit.

Resources

Dr. Christine Wood of Failure Analysis Associates.

"Parents and Grandparents: Poison-proof Your Home," from the Los Angeles Regional Poison Control Center.

WALKERS

More than three million walkers are sold in the United States every year, according to *Your Child's Wellness Newsletter*. Parents who use them say they help keep babies quiet and entertained, and even promote walking. And, except for the part about the walking, I haven't found any evidence to dispute these claims. The problem is that walkers also seem to promote serious injuries.

Every year, 27,500 children go to the emergency room to be treated for injuries that happened while they were in their walkers (being quiet and entertained). Here's the scenario: Mom, Dad, Grandma, or a sitter puts junior into the walker so he can play. Suddenly this baby, who normally can't stand reliably, let alone walk, has complete mobility, and hands-free height. He now requires lots more supervision than he normally would, because he can reach things and get into places he normally couldn't. But instead of supervising more, the caregiver has taken advantage of baby's distraction to turn their attention to other things—leaving the baby free to grab and go at will.

The supervising adult may even decide it's okay to run downstairs while baby is busy, leaving the baby gate temporarily open. This means the baby can try to follow—right down the stairs. (See also "Stairs.") Falling down stairs causes 80 percent of walker-related injuries, says the National Safe Kids Campaign.

This organization, along with the American Academy of Pediatrics, says walkers should be banned. Normally, I would say that this ruling was a little harsh, and that parents should just provide the necessary supervision to children in walkers. But in light of the number of injuries, and the fact that about 25 percent of them are severe fractures and head injuries, I'm joining the ban-the-walker camp.

Even well-educated, kid-conscious colleagues at *L.A. Parent* magazine have told me horror stories of a relative's child taking a header down the basement stairs and, thankfully, escaping with only two broken fingers. Another colleague, parented by a mother-of-the-year candidate, had her own baby teeth knocked out thanks to this rolling hazard.

If you want to keep your baby entertained, try Barney (at least he will do the child no *physical* harm). Or better yet, take a break and actually *play* with her. Save the walking for when she can walk.

Resources

"Walkers Take a Fall," *Your Child's Wellness Newsletter,* January/February 1996, volume 4, number 1.
"Falls" fact sheet, from the National Safe Kids Campaign; (202) 884-4993.

WATER

Water, water everywhere. But is it safe for your family to drink? The U.S. Centers for Disease Control reports that the health risks of bad drinking water in the United States are generally low—but rising.

Thanks to human sewage, industrial waste, pesticide runoff, leaching from municipal landfills, and leaking of pollutants from underground storage tanks containing everything from gasoline and oil to chemical and nuclear waste, your drinking water might not be as safe as you think, says *The Green Guide* in a recent issue on water quality.

Children are especially susceptible to the hazards of unsafe drinking water, because they drink more water than adults in relation to their body weight, and their bodies and immune systems are still developing, making it more difficult to fight of the bad effects of contaminants, according to J. Routt Reigart, M.D., past chair of the American Academy of Pediatrics Committee on Environmental Health.

Testing the waters

Because water quality varies from region to region, and from the source (well, reservoir, etc.) to the point of use (your tap), the only way for you to know for sure if your family's water is safe is to have it tested. Water companies are required by the Safe Drinking Water Act to test their water and report on its quality to the state and the Environmental Protection Agency. You can get a copy of these results by calling your water company.

This report, however, will not show any contaminants that enter the water between the treatment center and your home. It will not show asbestos from cement water mains, lead leached from service lines or plumbing, or bacteria growing in your hot-water tank or reservoirs between the facility and your tap. So you still need to follow up with a test from an EPA-certified private lab.

For help in getting test results from your water company, or in finding a certified lab to test your water, you can call the EPA Safe Drinking Water Hotline at (800) 426-4791. You can also contact Suburban Water Testing Labs at (800) 433-6595 or National Testing Labs at (800) 426-8378 to have your water tested by mail.

Water bugs

Your test results may show one, or a combination of several, contaminants in your water.

Bacteria and viruses can get into your water through human sewage or animal feces and can cause any number of diseases— dysentery, hepatitis, Legionnaires' disease, E.coli, etc. Water is generally disinfected with chlorine to kill these organisms. Cryptosporidium and *Giardia lambia,* however, are immune to chlorine, and can cause fatal illness in AIDS patients and people with weak immune systems (like infants and small children).

Lead can leach into your water from lead-lined pipes in or outside your home, or from copper pipes joined with lead soldering. More than half of U.S. cities still use these types of piping, and they are the most common source of lead in drinking water. Lead can cause severe developmental delays in children. (See "Lead.")

Organic compounds such as benzene, carbon tetrachloride, and vinyl chloride in water are believed to cause cancer, and can also damage the nervous system.

Arsenic gets into water near copper and iron smelting operations, and through its use as a wood preservative. It can lead to abnormal fetal development and heart disease.

Cadmium can leach out of pipes, and also gets into the water through leaking landfills and fertilizer runoff. Exposure is associated with hypertension and kidney damage.

Asbestos can leach into the water from cement water mains. (See "Asbestos.")

Cyanide in water is the result of insecticide runoff, metal refining, and plastics manufacturing.

Nitrates are most common in farm-area water supplies. They come from nitrogen fertilizers and can enter municipal water supplies through farm runoff. They are associated with "blue-baby syndrome" in infants, because they disrupt the blood's ability to carry oxygen.

Organic chemicals such as atrazine and alachlor (both pesticides), dioxins and PCBs (industrial chemicals), and styrene (from plastics) are notorious in the Midwest, Louisiana, and the Chesapeake Bay region. All are associated with increased cancer risk and other health problems.

Chlorine is added to all municipal water supplies to disinfect, but it can react with organic chemicals to form new chemicals that are associated with rectal, bladder, and pancreatic cancer, and may cause birth defects.

Water purification

The contaminants you find in your water will help determine the way you go about making it safer.

Bottled water may seem like the quick and easy way to keep the family safe. But a 1991 analysis of thirty-nine bottled waters at the University of Iowa found such contaminants as nitrates, arsenic, and high levels of bacteria in some of these products, and concluded that bottled water was not significantly better or worse than the tap water in that state. And the International Bottled Water Association reports that about 25 percent of water bottled in the United States is simply treated city water.

If you want to ensure you're getting safe bottled water, ask questions before you buy.

Dispensing machines, found at most supermarkets, are usually just hooked directly into the municipal water supply and run through a filter, distiller, or disinfector in the machine. Find out from the vending company or the supermarket manager exactly what kinds of filtration is used (a combination of several is best) and how often the filters are serviced.

If you're going to have your water delivered, have the company send you a breakdown of mineral and contamination content, find out the sources of the water, and ask how often and by whom the water is tested. The testing organization should be certified by an independent organization like the National Sanitation Foundation International. You should also ask if the company imports water from other sources when its normal source cannot meet demands.

You can **flush out** much of the lead that might be in your tap water by letting the water run for a few minutes—especially first thing in the morning. This gets rid of the water that has been sitting in your pipes, and is more likely to contain lead leached from the pipes. Use only cold water for drinking and cooking, since hot water is more likely to pick up lead from the pipes.

To get rid of chlorine and its by-products, you can **let water**

stand in an open pitcher in the refrigerator for a few days before drinking or using it to mix punch or juice. The chlorine will evaporate away.

Boiling your water before drinking, or especially before using it to mix infant formula, will get rid of bacteria, viruses and other organizms that might be present. The American Academy of Pediatrics even recommends boiling bottled water before giving it to infants. But don't overboil. Too much boiling can increase the concentration of lead in the water.

Filters

Several types of home water-filtration systems are now available to improve the qualtiy of the water coming from your tap.

Carbon filters can reduce the amount of chlorine, pesticides, and organic chemicals in the water, and can eliminate unpleasant tastes and odors. There are a variety of sizes available, from those that connect straight to the tap to those that filter through the supply pipes.

Distillation systems actually boil your water for you, and then collect the condensed steam, which is then free of minerals, salts, and suspended solids.

Ultraviolet disinfection systems use UV rays to kill microorganisms present in the water. They do not, however, filter out chemicals or solid material, and must by used in conjunction with other systems.

Reverse osmosis systems filter water through a semipermeable membrane that stops microorganisms, chemicals, and solids from passing through.

Whatever system you select, you should check to see that it is certified by either the Water Quality Association ([708] 505-0160) or NSF International ([313] 769-8010) to remove the specific contaminants you are concerned about.

Resources

"Toxins on Tap," by Wendy Gordon, M.S., *The Green Guide,* July 14, 1996, number 27.

"Is Your Tap Water Safe?" *Your Child's Wellness Newsletter,* Summer 1996, volume 4, number 2.

Consumer's Guide to Protecting the Water Your Family Drinks, from Kinetico, Inc., makers of RO filtration systems; (800) 944-WATER; http://www.kinetico.com.

WINDOWS

If the weather is warm, it's nice to have an open window to bring in the breeze—and a fresh supply is good for your home's indoor air quality. But open windows, if not properly protected, are a serious threat to young children.

Catching falls

Falls from windows kill about eighteen children under age ten a year, and injured 4,700 kids under age fourteen in 1993. One of the best known tragedies involving a fall from a window is the case of Connor, the four-year-old son of popular musician Eric Clapton, who died in a fall from the window of his mother's Manhattan high-rise apartment in 1992, prompting Clapton to write the Grammy-winning song "Tears in Heaven."

But don't think your child is safe just because you live in a one- or two-story house. Almost 90 percent of children injured in window falls in 1993 fell from a height of two stories or less.

To make your windows safer, consider installing window guards—especially if you live two stories or more off the ground. If you live in an apartment with children, your landlord may be required to install window guards for you. Call your city hall to find out. Don't rely on screens to keep children safe, warns the National Safe Kids Campaign. They aren't strong enough to prevent children from falling through. It's also a good idea to keep all furniture a good distance away from windows so children won't be tempted to climb up.

If window guards are out of the question for you, simple devices are available at most hardware stores that allow the window to be opened a few inches and then locked. Just make sure you don't leave an unprotected window open more than three or four inches. The National Safe Kids Campaign says windows open even five inches are dangerous to kids under ten. Leaving the window open this wide could let a child's body through, but trap her head and strangle her.

Cutting the cord

Another danger from windows is that children can be strangled by the cords from curtains or blinds. Almost two hundred children have died this way since 1981, according to the Consumer Product Safety Commission. Younger victims, usually ten to fifteen months old, generally reach the cords from cribs that are placed near windows. Older children, ages two to four, usually find the cords hanging near the floor or get tangled in them when they climb up on a nearby piece of furniture to look out the window.

To keep cords safer in horizontal blinds or pleated shades, cut the cord above the tassel so there is no loop for your child to get tangled in. If you don't like the look of this, install separate tassels at the end of each cord. For vertical blinds, continuous loop systems, or drapery cords, permanently attach a cord tie-down device to the floor, wall, or window jamb.

Free tassels and tie-down devices are available by calling the Window Covering Safety Council at (800) 506-4636.

As a temporary quick fix, you might use a twist tie or a clothespin to roll up dangling cords and secure them out of reach of your child. This may be too inconvenient to be used permanently, however, because you have to make sure those cords are well out of your child's reach *every time* you open or close the drapes or blinds. This is another good reason to keep furniture away from windows.

Resources

"Children Can Strangle in Window Covering Cords," from the U.S. Consumer Product Safety Commission; (800) 638-2772.

"Falls" fact sheet and "Falls Prevention" tip sheet, from the National Safe Kids Campaign.

"Preventing Kids' Falls Is a Matter of Physics," by Laurence G. Proulx, *The Washington Post*, January 31, 1995.

YARD

If you are lucky enough to have a house with a yard, you have a chance to create a safe area where your children can play at almost any time and enjoy the great outdoors.

Fencing

The best way to make sure your child stays safely within the safe haven you've created is to have a fence around your yard. If your yard isn't fenced, set clear limits on where your child is allowed to play. Make them simple to understand—the edge of the lawn or the edge of the driveway—so that your child will have no trouble remembering.

Of course, you can't count on either clear boundaries or fences alone to keep your child safe. You or another responsible adult should always be nearby to supervise outdoor play.

Play structures

If you're going to set up play equipment for your child, such as a swing set or climbing structure, choose and install it carefully, and make sure it is surrounded by proper protective surfacing. (See "Playgrounds.")

Pools

If there is a pool in your yard, it should be completely surrounded by a nonclimbable fence that is at least five feet high. The gate should be kept shut and locked at all times when the pool is not in use. If the fence doesn't separate the pool area from the house, then all doors leading to the pool area should be locking and alarmed. (See "Swimming.")

Plants

Be careful which plants you choose to landscape your yard. Some are poisonous. If there are plants you're not sure about, take a sample to your nursery or call your local poison control center. (See "Plants.")

Yard work

Most of the things that make your yard beautiful can be dangerous to your children.

If you use fertilizers or pesticides, read and follow the manufacturer's instructions carefully. Once you have applied the chemical in question, don't let your children play in the yard again until it is safe to do so. Better yet, try one of the nontoxic pesticides or fertilizers on the market today. And be sure to store all types of lawn-care products in their original containers, where you are sure your child cannot get at them.

Mowers, trimmers, and other gardening equipment should never be used when children are in the area. These products are dangerous, causing about 400,000 emergency-room visits every year, according to the Consumer Product Safety Commission. The blades of a typical power lawn mower rotate at three thousand revolutions per minute, and many of the seventy-five thousand injuries they cause every year are to children, according to *Your Child's Wellness Newsletter*.

Make sure your children are indoors, with adult supervision, before turning on any piece of garden equipment. Continue to be on the lookout while you are mowing, trimming, etc., and turn the equipment off the minute a child comes into the area. Never give your child a ride on a ride-on mower. According to the Outdoor Power Equipment Institute, these devices are designed with safety features that protect the operator, but are not built for passengers. Fifteen children are killed every year when they get into the path of these mowers, according to the CPSC.

Turn power tools of all kinds off and make them inoperable whenever you are not using them, and store them out of children's reach. Children should never be allowed to operate gardening equipment of any kind until they are at least fourteen years old.

Patio furniture

Yard and garden furniture should be chosen carefully if children are around. Some types of lightweight plastic furniture aren't very sturdy and could easily tip over under the weight of a climbing child. Folding metal lounge chairs can pinch, or even sever, little fingers. And hammocks without spreader bars (which spread out the mesh part of the hammock) are a strangulation hazard.

Barbecues

The easiest way to protect your children from barbecue accidents is to make sure they are supervised indoors when the barbecue is hot. This is especially important when you are lighting the barbecue, because the children might also distract you and cause you to injure yourself.

If you do have children present while you are using the barbecue, set clear boundaries concerning how close to the grill they are allowed. Explain that even after the food is off, the grill will still be hot, and they shouldn't touch or go near it. Make sure that while you are cooking, another adult is present with the direct responsibility of supervising the children and making sure they keep at a safe distance.

Resources

"Lawn and Garden Safety Tips," from the U.S. Consumer Product Safety Commission.

"Careless Mowing Habits Could Lead Children Down a Dangerous Path," from the Outdoor Power Equipment Institute, 341 South Patrick St., Alexandria, VA 22314.

"Lawn Mower Injuries in Children," *Your Child's Wellness Newsletter*, November/December 1995.

ENDNOTE

If you've made it all the way to the end of this book, chances are you're pretty nervous. But don't read *Safe and Secure* as a laundry list of bad things that could happen to your child. There is plenty you can do to make sure your kids stay safe, and most of it is common sense. The big dangers are obvious, and the small dangers are, well, small.

Chances are excellent that you were well equipped to keep your children out of harm's way before you even opened this book. You love your kids, and want them to grow into safe, happy adults. The details I've provided in *Safe and Secure* aren't meant to scare you into locking your family away from fun. Think of this book as a handy guide you can use to take constructive preventive measures. Then you can spend less time worrying about your kids, and more time enjoying the fun of being a parent.